NOTES FROM THE BONFIRE

POEMS IN THE AGE OF CORONAVIRUS

MATT NAGIN

WITH PHOTOGRAPHS BY ANDRZEJ JERZY LECH AND ILLUSTRATIONS BY NATASHA YEARWOOD

Notes From The Bonfire

Poems in the Age of Coronavirus

by

Matt Nagin

With photographs by Andrzej Jerzy Lech

and illustrations by Natasha Yearwood

Published by Burning Flower Press

Drawings by Natasha Yearwood

Photographs by Andrzej Jerzy Lech

ISBN: 978-0-578-79621-5

PREVIOUSLY PUBLISHED

Postcards and *We Go On* were published in *Gravitas*

The Virus That Hunted The Sun was published as *Covid-19* in *Poetry In The Time of Coronavirus*

When The World Ended was published in *Coronavirus Anthology 2*

Yes was published in *The Organic Poet*

BOOKS BY MATT NAGIN

Do Not Feed The Clown, Tenth Street Press

Feast of Sapphires, Burning Flower Press

Butterflies Lost Within The Crooked Moonlight, Burning Flower Press

From The Fridge To The Crackerjack Box, Burning Flower Press

* * *

PRAISE FOR FEAST OF SAPPHIRES

"Nagin feels his work, writing it with gritted teeth, through a pen as sharp as a razor, and his cynicism is smart and infectious. Poetry of the highest quality."

—MATT MCAVOY, MATT MCAVOY'S REVIEWS

"A poetic feast as surprising as it is satisfying."

—KIRKUS REVIEW

"With his poetry, Matt Nagin seeks to inform, infiltrate, and discover the mind, and does so with a very human and caring heart. I thoroughly recommend this collection of poetry and consider it to be one of the best I've read in a while." (5 stars)

—P.D. DAWSON

"If you are a lover of poetry, you'll really enjoy what's inside this book."

—LISA BINION, LISA'S WRITOPIA

PRAISE FOR BUTTERFLIES LOST WITHIN THE CROOKED MOONLIGHT

"Kerouac and Ginsberg also understood poetry as effusion, and Nagin seems to have learned much from these countercultural icons. Powerful verse from

a writer of real talent."

—KIRKUS REVIEWS

"More personal than W.H. Auden (The Shield Of Achilles), more gut-wrenching than Robert Frost (The Lovely Shall Be Choosers). Dystopian power in forty-five poems."

—JIM BENNETT, JIM BENNETT REVIEWS (5 STARS)

"The inner chatter of a conflicted, incongruous – and brilliant – mind."

—BILL GARRY, BILL GARRY'S REVIEWS

"Nagin delivers in stark and jarring completeness."

– ERIN NICHOLE COCHRAN, READERS' FAVORITE (5 STARS)

CONTENTS

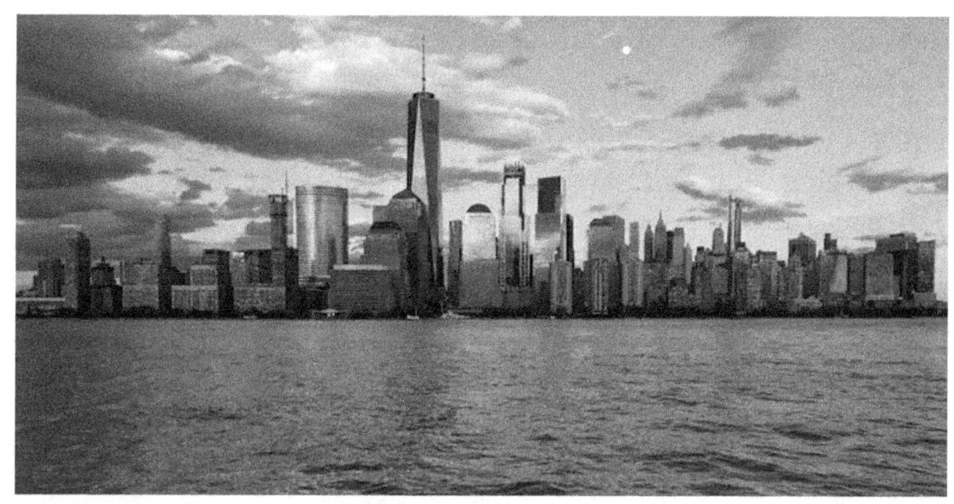

PROLOGUE

I've been a New York City resident for twenty years. On 9/11, I watched the towers burn from 14th Street and 7th Avenue. Smoke billowed towards us, crowds fleeing. I've been involved in Occupy Wall Street Protests, Anti-Iraq War protests, two strikes at Long Island University's Brooklyn Campus, Halloween Parades, Mermaid Parades, The Hare Krishna Festival in Washington Square Park, you name it. As a comedian, I've crisscrossed the city endless times, performing at every club in the NYC metro area, as well as running from one acting audition to the next, or hurrying to teach a class.

New York City is my home. It is what I know. It is what I grew accustomed to above and beyond anything else. Still, what I know —what I considered my sanctuary—was hurled into a maelstrom. Covid-19. The pandemic sent countless residents fleeing, infecting others till it became the epicenter of the U.S. outbreak. The government dropped the ball, in many ways, President Trump, at first, at least, suggesting it would disappear like magic. The CDC, meanwhile, not only bungled early tests, they claimed it could only be spread by respiratory droplets (such as from a cough). In fact, the virus was fully airborne and way more contagious than the flu.

On an immuno-suppressant for Crohn's disease, I was one of the more vulnerable. Just my luck: I was also one of the first to get it. I suspect the source was my girlfriend, as she and her relatives all came down with it. Then again, it could have been my brother, who got sick with a fever and a bad cough after a trip to Japan. The truth is I'll never know. The virus is so contagious you could literally get it anywhere.

Regardless, it was a tremendous struggle. I have asthma. This magnified any minor breathing issues I had exponentially. Countless nights I could not get sufficient oxygen. I'd be wheezing, feeling lightheaded, the breathing issues not responding to my inhaler. I was put on Prednisone, from a City MD, which barely helped.

I had chest pains. Fever. Headaches that lasted days and did not respond to Tylenol. Meanwhile, I've always been sensitive to sound, but with coronavirus, my noisy neighbors were driving me nuts. I'd previously asked them to keep it down to no avail, so I paced back and forth in my tiny studio apartment, banging a broomstick against the wall. I also started making holes in the ceiling. When this didn't help, I lugged around a hammer, thinking of beating down the wall with it.

I felt like Jack Nicholson in the scene in *The Shining* where he keeps throwing the curb ball against the wall. That out of sorts. I'd been to the doctor, but had yet to get my results, at this point, although I was under a 14-day quarantine as a precautionary measure. In the interest of preserving my sanity, I put on an N-95 mask and some gloves, rented a car, and fled to my parent's house on Long Island (they were in Florida).

There I had plenty of free time—while under quarantine—and —though I landed in the E.R. once with breathing issues—and needed two asthma medicines and a much higher dose of Prednisone as well as a course of Azithromycin—after around a month I was out on the other side. I had beaten Covid-19. Still, every day I watched the news and learned of people like me, often younger than me, who had succumbed to the virus. My heart went out to their families. The tragedy was unthinkable.

I determined to write about what had happened to our world in the best way I know how: through a poetic lens. This seemed the most sensible way to respond to all the death and suffering. If these poems sound dark, it is because the world has become this way. If they sound bitter, it is not because I feel this way, so much as that I've tried to view matters as unfiltered as possible.

There are other poems here; poems about abortion, poems about the creative process, poems about shooting turtles in Alabama, but the main emphasis here are poems that deal—in some sense—with the crushing pandemic that has radically altered our world.

To be honest, I've always had an apocalyptic vision. Doomsday poems are the way I think, generally. Don't get me wrong. I'm not a tin foil hat guy. Still, I do venture into these maudlin spaces, and, psychologically speaking, at least, identify with those who feel the sky is falling.

I hope these poems can be of some help to others. Perhaps they can even provide new ways to process what we've all been through. Regardless, I felt compelled to write them. They are records of my attempt to deal honestly with the sense of loss and powerlessness, to search, among the shadows, for the briefest glimmer of hope.

I've been through a lot over the years. Three major surgeries for Crohn's disease, getting hit by a car crossing the street (that required years of physical therapy), Covid-19, numerous intestinal obstructions etc. All of this is not even to mention the countless romantic relationships that went sour, the lost teaching jobs, the family struggles, the endless rejection in the entertainment industry.

Still, I've kept going. Certainly, writing this book helped. So come along. Check it out. What, really, do you have to lose?

—Matt Nagin
03/29/2020

THE VIRUS THAT HUNTED THE SUN

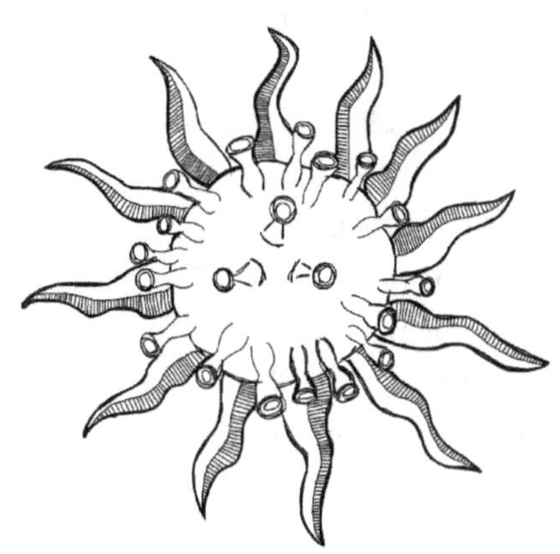

Scrap your plans, brother.
Maniacs are throwing it all
out the window,
wall street sharks
are putting a little extra grease
in the funky hair,
a tire lady
starts selling her cough
instead of her sorrow,
the functionary on TV
is droning on about
selling your bonds—
the value of a lifetime—
as the NBA is shut down.

Broadway is a ghost town.
Flights out of JFK to Puerto Rico
go for 21$,
and all flights from Europe
are banned for thirty days—
value of a lifetime.
Great deal.
Get in while you can.
Thanks Jim Cramer,
any other great advice?

Meanwhile, I'm on the couch
choking,
my chest killing
my fever high.
Meanwhile, I'm quarantined
the neighbor banging on

the godforsaken wall,
the ceiling collapsing
the night turning
into a tornado.
Meanwhile, I'm spitting
into the eye of my fate
and trying to laugh
and laugh
and laugh—
and tell myself
this is just a silly dream.

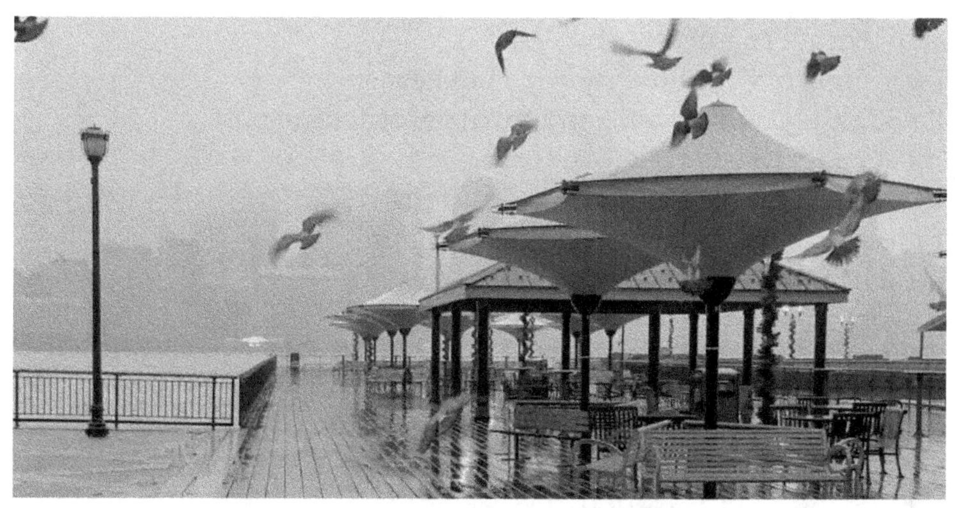

POSTCARD

Great to get that postcard, Jerry.
Thrilled you are well and losing
weight by going paleo—yeehaw!—
a diet based on cavemen who foraged
for berries and hunted beasts makes
perfect sense. Anyway, listen, I'm gonna
sell a plot of land and take up ice fishing
or just check out early and bum around...
rrrroom rrroom rrroom...maybe hit a few
strip clubs or get lost in the Adirondacks...
doesn't really matter, Jerry, we're all
entering the sinkhole, the virus is
spreading and I'm fairly certain the
final rainbow is just around the bend.

So Jerry...Jerry ol buddy, just know this
life feels too short...zzzzipp zzzaap...
it's over in a cinch, see? You got nothing
to show for it but maybe a plot of land
where you can be buried and some
writings no one will ever read, hahaha.

Still, I don't regret any of it—and if
I fell short of my mark so be it...I'm here,
I'm kicking...whappoo!...and spiritual teachings
by gurus can only take you so far,
even if it is Buddhism which allows the
follower to really stick to a protocol and
relies on meditation, which is sort of a
science in a way....

What I'm trying to say is...oh geez...
I miss those early days, those
carefree times, and I'd give anything
for one more loop around, if you get me,
one more rodeo, man, but these look like
the twilight years and I gotta make peace
with it...oh boy...and look towards that
godforsaken setting sun...since you never
know when the darkness will be here...and...
goddamnit...well heck man...whazoo!...I had
some hell of adventures, really raced towards
the sun, if you get what I mean, so there's that,
and the knowledge that I'm still at this...still kicking,
yo...still in some crazy way...got a chance.

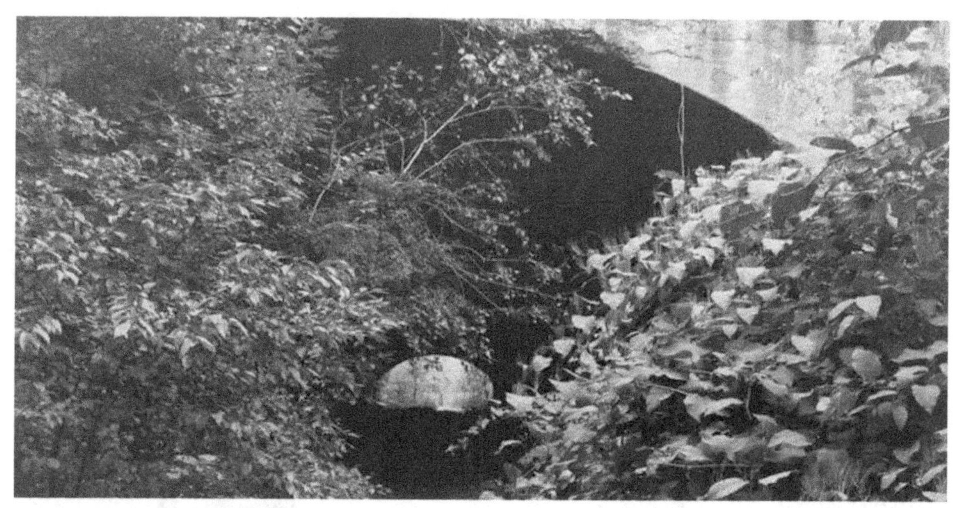

WE GO ON

We go on; persevere; sing through
tunnels of desperation; fly backwards
imploding—wings at the threshold—
flames eating promise—we flood
the vacant night—burn ambition—
and when the rollercoaster whirls
into the depths of the sky we sink—
collapsing—the fences are barns—
the burnings are just angels
praying for all that has been lost.

Go on—we—kites into atmospheres—
lava into the vibrant city—smoke
rushing to save the bible from itself—
jagged parables—metaphors that
break—on—go—we—a hawk in a
cauldron, the zenith among endless
rats, twisting—always contorting—
as we—yes—we—go on.

PRAYER OF THE ATHEIST

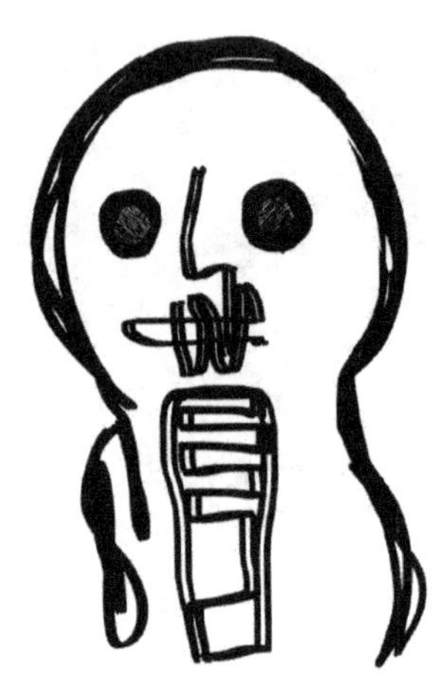

Crush the night like a plague.
Sing in forgotten woods.
Masquerade where no routes
seem possible.

To be an anti-influencer. Slide
down the wrong chute. Fire.
Snails in a pit. A house
crushed under the weight
of broken dreams.

Tricked by love.
Consumed by forgetting.
Reach. Hurt. The hammer resonating.
A lightning bolt. A curse where
all you need is prayer.

Do you hear me, God? Will
you hold my hand?
Will you grasp the ways I
crisscrossed into the bog
of my own defeat?
I'm sorry. I messed up.
Took the easy route.
Forgot what really mattered.

The ceiling entranced.
Stars weeping on my shoes.
Hello? Anyone there?
Ash tray. Coffin. A limerick
that goes on and on.

Anyone? ANYONE?

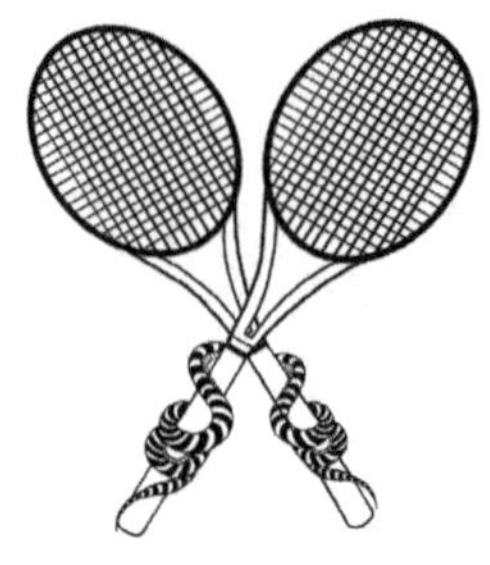

GAME. SET. MATCH.

My profile is set to private
so I can keep the stalkers at bay;
and my heart is set to expire
so the sea can drown me;
and a leopard eat the spots
in his fur
as if set for new parameters;
my opponent on the tennis court
is ready to serve me up
make me
ready—entirely—
for game set match.

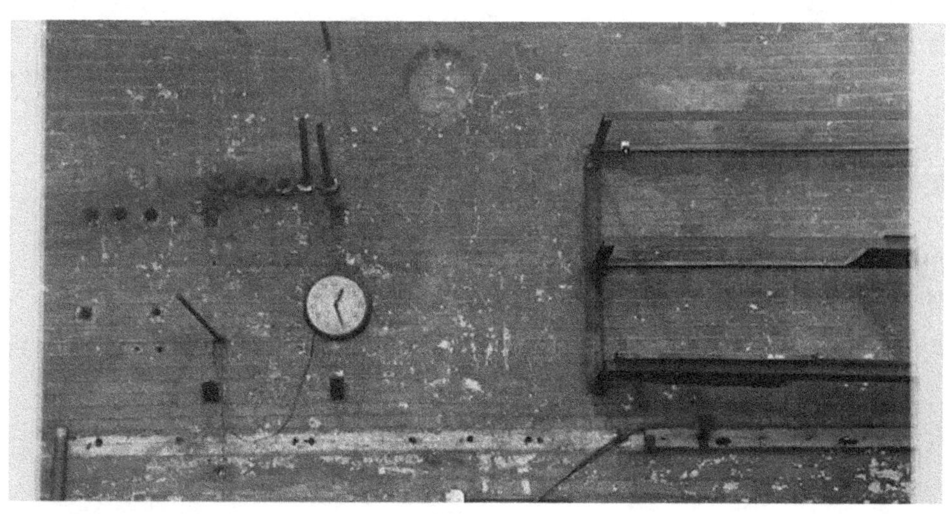

DEATH TO MATT JR.

I'm sorry little buddy
my friend whirling back
here from an alien land;
you were in the womb
of my beloved
kicking with that
trembling little foot;
you were in the stars
of my radiant heaven,
giggling and sucking
on the old thumb;
you were a representation
of me, the spirit of
my becoming; you were
the face of the future,
the genetic sprawl,
you were ambition
splashed across
the universe and
I wanted to hug you
and throw a ball with you

and teach you what counts.

But now I'm sorry little buddy,
little Matt Jr.,
I'm sorry about what we're gonna
do to you;
I'm sorry we're gonna take it
all away before it even starts;
I'm sorry for your early demise.

You could have been an Einstein
a Freud, a Picasso;
you could have puked into
the atmosphere a melody
of pure gold;
you could have danced
with eternity
and melted the sky
so that all was molten
and reflected back in your image;
you could have made me so
goddamn proud.

I'm sorry I'm not ready.
I'm sorry I'm taking the easy way out.
I'm sorry I didn't love you enough
or give you that fighting chance.
I'm sorry but we're headed to the
abortion clinic,
gonna have you vacuumed away.

I'm sorry for that,
your death
no way to account for it,
or justify it;
I'm really sorry;
but one day

I'll have another son like you
and I'll treat him damn well
and make up for this moment.

One day I'll be a hell of a father;
I'm sorry it's not to you,
but those seem to be the
cards you've been dealt,
and it wouldn't have been
good anyway
without my heart
fully in it—
but, yes,
I'm sorry, goddamnit,
sorry beyond words.

I'M ALIVE

Matters turn grim,
the enemy seizes
your crown,
a trapeze artist
falls
into
blankets
of
forgetting.

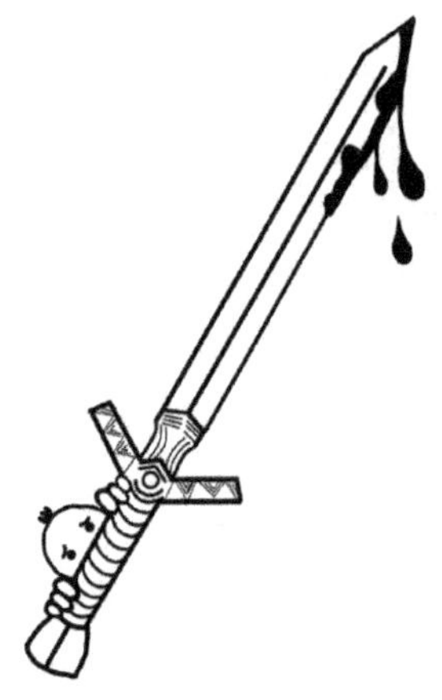

And?
So?
I'M ALIVE!

Say it—
those magic
words
syllables
catapulting you
into the
next sphere;
Kubrick, Dickinson,
Swift, Bukowski, Cervantes;
all your heroes—regardless of
the magic they created—in spite of
the many ways they inspired—
DEAD—

and though the frog boils
and the nights no
longer scream—
and though the magic
slips out a back entrance
and the kite has no man

to control the string—
and though the years
slip through uneasy fingers
and the electric afternoon
becomes a gale of ice
as the lions feast
on your dreams—

say it with me
be thankful for it
embrace it
consecrate it
I'M ALIVE!

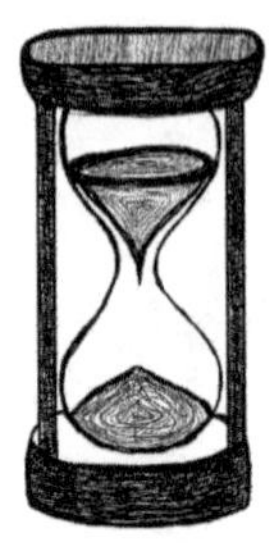

TIME LEFT

I used to think there
was so much more
to go—that we could
swim forever in
choppy seas—that
the party wasn't close
to finished, that I had so
much time left; but now
I'm on the dessert course,
the night is a scarecrow,
love has his eyes carved out,
reforms are a broomstick
in flame, and everyone is
swing dancing, man,
pretending the final curtain
isn't just around the corner.

Every last window is being broken,
the clocks keep winding down
and it's sad how little time is left,
how we pretend this is
not what is going on
as the dreams implode

wild accomplishments fade
and all of it
just so quickly
slips away.

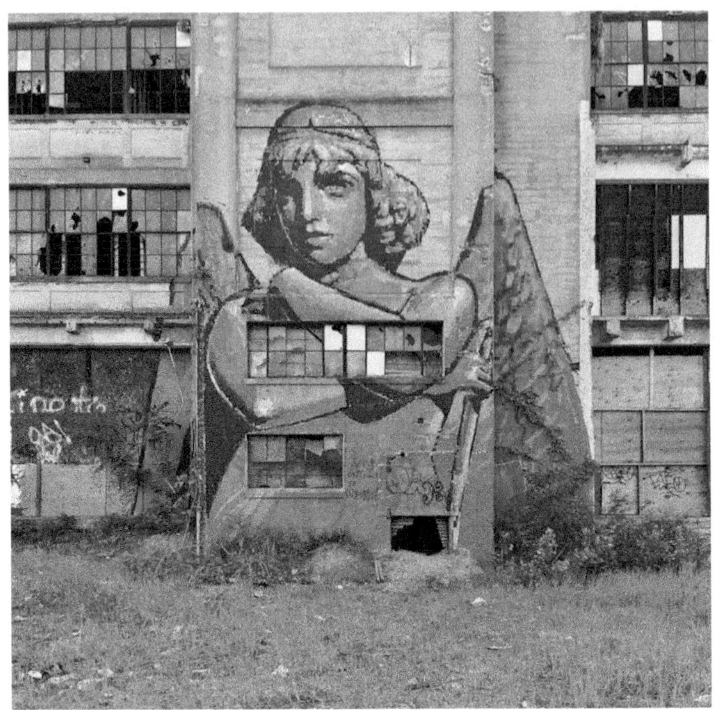

I LOST

Ok. I lost.
Take my car keys.
Here is the password to my safe.

You want my warm bed?
A reason to live?
You want to sprinkle
this magic light all over
your frosted flakes?
You want the source
of my eternal joy,
the fire of my creative engine?
Or my heart on a bed of
leafy greens?

Ok. I got mixed up in the wrong jam.

I got my career stuck in
a busted sink. Wasted decades.
Never quite found enough love.
Never finished those novels.
Managed to flub every opportunity,
neglected to demonstrate sufficient gratitude
when the heavens rained
such bounty upon me.

Ok. Fine. I'm a screwup.
Never lived up to the hype
or found a way to bring the lightning
upon command,
messed up every relationship,
only knew how to love myself first,
was too blind to the pain of others,
too distracted by a billion foolish needs.

Ok, I was vain.
Ok, I was cowardly.
Ok, I didn't have quite the right work ethic
and wasted years just thinking
it would all magically work out.

Ok, I rang the wrong buzzer
let racoons into my house
fell into a manhole
sang to the wrong sun.

Ok. Ok. It wasn't good enough.
It wasn't what you wanted.

But I'm here now goddamnit,
and I'm ready to turn this
big old bus around,
so sit back
and watch
as my crazy ass

makes up
for lost time.

LET THE WORDS OUT LIKE RAIN

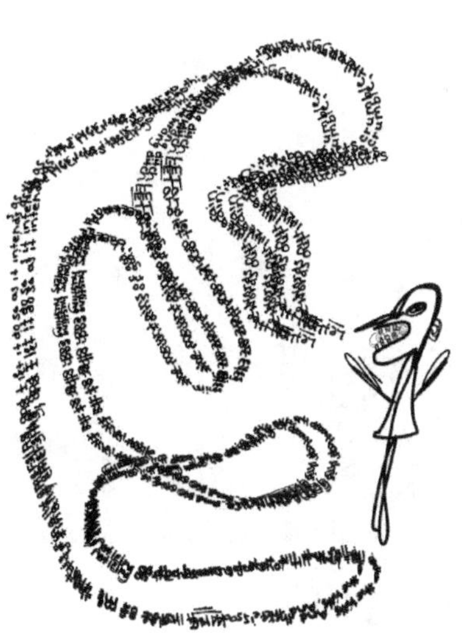

Let the words out like rain,
the banquets crumble,
the kings wander into the wrong
ditch.

Let and let and let and there are
eyes
in the mountains of god,
backward players hustling each
other
at the final table,
a dog who is dying every day
of his goddamn life.

And no one is stopping
or in any way noticing
as the heavens get shot
till they fall into the hills.

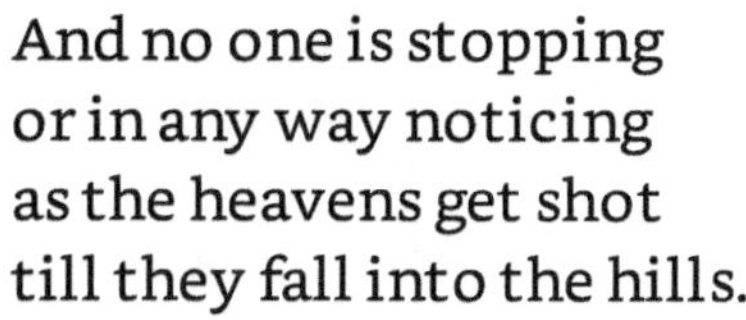

And there is a king inside of me
that is finally emerging,
and I let it develop as it intends
as the river lets itself go this way and that
all natural and along a course already set for it
or a robin flies off towards some new adventure
blissfully unaware of the arrow that seeks it from afar.

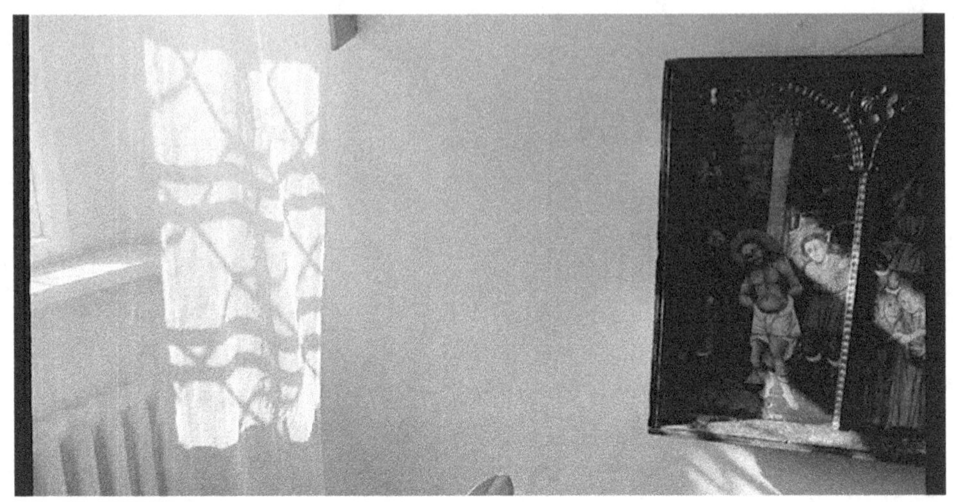

UPDATE

How you doing?

I'm hanging off the edge of the earth,
swimming in cesspools of my own ambition.

How you managing?

I'm in the muck of a recovery
that never ends
playing games
when I could be
marching forward
like Spartacus with
that fearless and bold plunge.

How you handling it all?

I got one hand in the toilet
of my own failures
and the other signaling
haphazardly to an indifferent god,
and I lost my keys
so that no door will ever open for me

in quite the same way again.

How you holding up?

I'm axing down redwood trees
and speaking in tongues
and my delirium is like a curse
that will never end.

Anything else?

Ha! Please. I'm just getting STARTED!

REALLY NICE KID

He is a really nice kid
and somehow it will work out for him,
cerebral palsy,
does not really grasp the extent of
his own defeat,
thinks the women love him when he
is only shunned
and all the jokers laugh behind his back.

He's a really nice kid,
though he can't shoot very well
at basketball
and half his body
the left side
just doesn't work right
and the jokes will come
the condescending sneers
given the awkward way he talks—
as if he could control it
as if preying upon the weak
was in any way fair—
and a week after staying at my house
he texts me "how are you?"
So I tell him my bad news
and he barely knows me
but says "I'm here for you."

He's a really nice kid—
someone with compassion
someone with that human touch—
a kid who can empathize
perhaps because of all
he's endured;
women won't see him that way,

employers will reject him,
he'll get boxed into a corner
and mocked for superficial reasons—
and I feel so bad, so awful
since he was always picked on
and will continue to face these
slings and arrows,
give so much
get so little in return,
but that's sort of your fate
I guess,
all you can expect
when you're
a really nice kid.

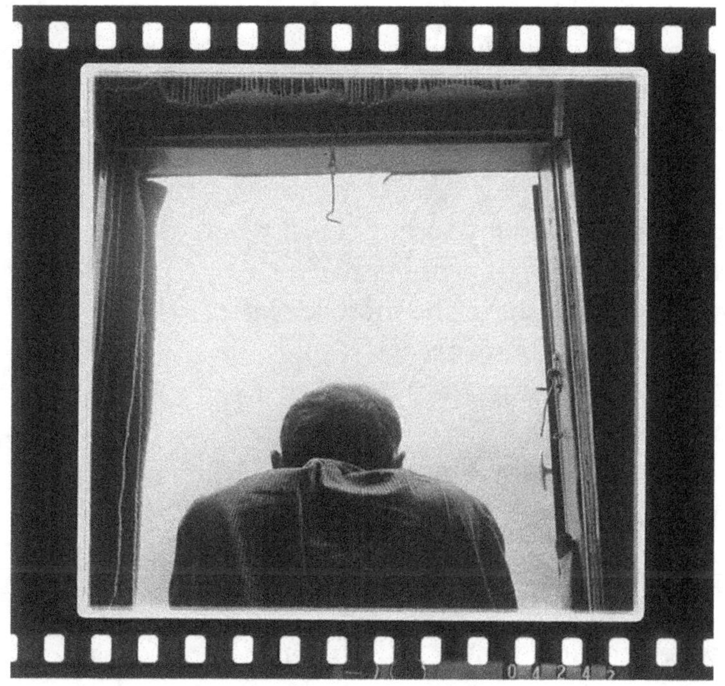

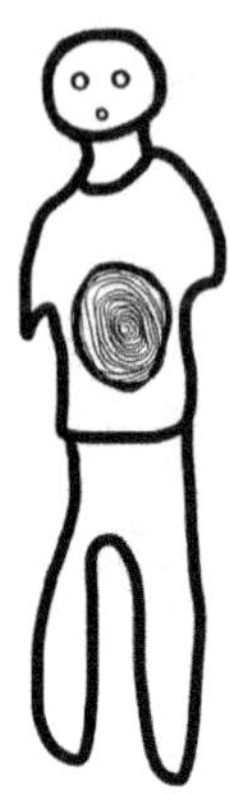

SOMETHING LEFT

There has to be something left inside me,
some sort of jewel to plunder—
I watch shows like *Shark Tank*—
I study the accomplishments of the many—
I wake up early and apply moisturizer—
I discipline myself like a monk.

There has to be some way to hug the sky
or at least feel a sense of progress,
some trigger point where the mojo kicks in,
some kite for new adventures,
some unlocked treasure
or potential solution
for so much sadness and dismay.

There has to be a secret path up the mountain,
or a code I have yet to break,
or hope when on a bed of knives,
or love when the loneliness is like a cage.

There has to be some bonus round,
some archetype I finally confront,
some book I wrangle out of the
inferno of endless defeat.
There has to be a love I still can find
when wandering these barren glaciers,
this vast lunar hell;
there has to be some sort of eagle taking off
from the furnace of Earth,
some pyramid in my honor,
some psalm yet to fall from my lips,
some way to grasp who I am,
tackle a dream, remember what counts.

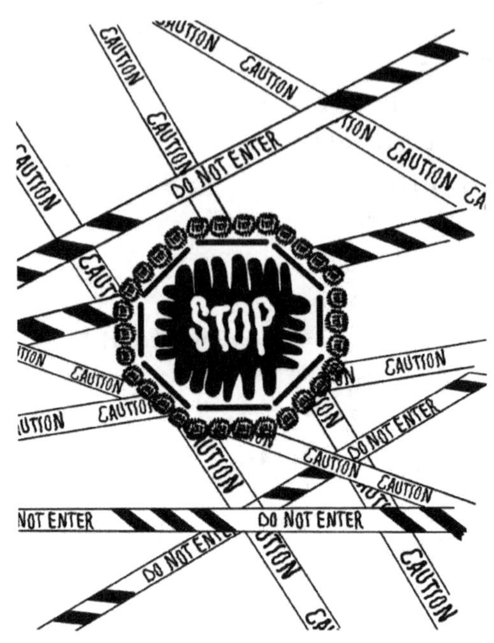

STOPS

Stops—everywhere you look—
gatekeepers—erect—monuments—
keep the wily—on the perimeter—
—barricades—fences—checkpoints—
barbed wire—boundaries—
Do Not Enter—Beware Of Dog.

They try so hard to keep you from
running in the dandelions—or building up
your destiny—they try so hard to twist you up
into such silly putty—stops—walls—
alarm systems—gates—blockades—
security clearances—the wolves circling
at the entrance.

They want you to sink into yourself—forget
you have a voice—cut off your radiance—
box you—shrink you—degrade your ambitions—

always judging—supercilious monsters—
overshadowing all progress while drinking
daquiris and admiring the scenic view.

Stops—military zones—buttressed walkways—
reinforced steel—scanners—bomb-sniffing dogs—
I.D. checking bastards looking at you as if you're
about to hijack a plane.

Sink into the reservoir—examine the limelight—
abandon fear—and make this the stop that counts—
the ultimate leap ahead into vast expanses—
canyons of radiance—flowing rivers of magical
heroic rebellion—stops—hahaha—not anymore;
not the same way; the red light is your signal
to go barreling ahead into the forbidden void.

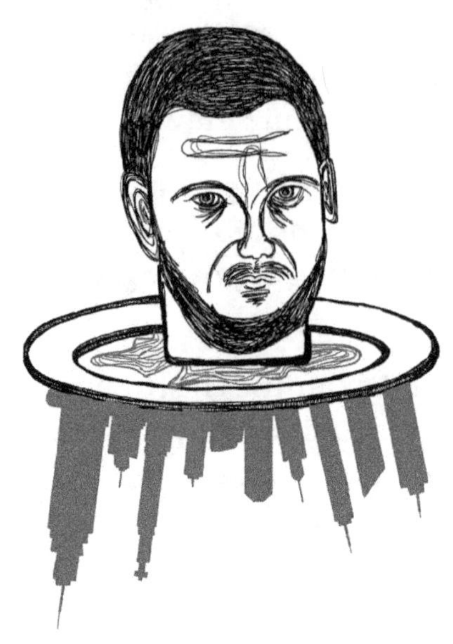

NEW YORK

The city eats me—
turns my brain into a cascade
of mutant worms—
sends daggers flying
into the soul of a rainbow.

The city is a marauder—
unleashing tortures—
plotting sinister revenge—
each of us squirming
as we struggle for air.

Smog for breakfast—
hookers for enlightenment—
trash receptacles overloaded
with mutant remains—
rats scurrying incessantly
along the same tracks.

The city eats me until I become
the banquet—
my soul on fine china—
tourists devouring
the emeralds of my desire.

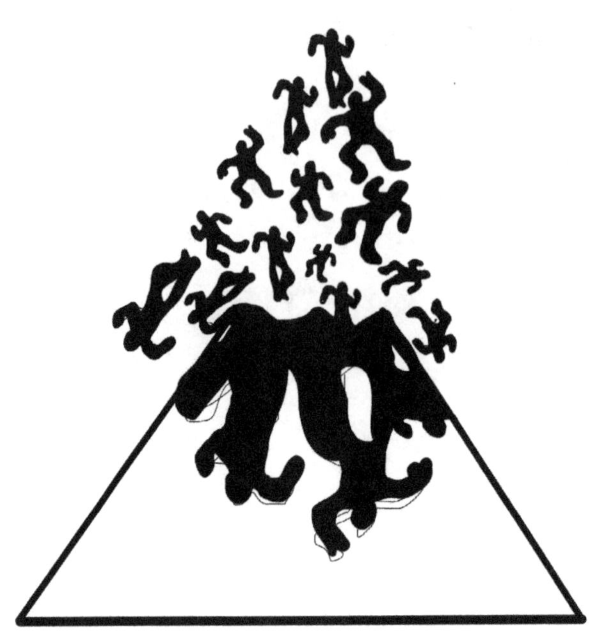

A THOUSAND DEATHS PER DAY

A thousand deaths per day
bodies stacked to the sky,
freezer trucks pulling up,
cemeteries filled to the brim,
actuaries freaking out
about endless
insurance claims.

What happened to
these bodies? Who are
these faceless masses?
What happened to these
gentle spirits? How can so many
American lives so rapidly
be taken away?

A thousand deaths per day;

mothers, grandmas and sons,
brothers, aunts and friends;
we're doing well, we're told, it could
have been worse—maybe 400k dead
when we're all done—we're really
accomplishing now—and when we
get our economy going—wow!—
what pent up demand!—gotta be
hopeful—think positive—we can
nip this pandemic in the bud—
drug treatments—vaccines—and I
hear all this—and I listen till it becomes
white noise—since all that matters—
all I can focus on—all that drowns out the glitter
and hocus pocus—is the tragedy—the absurdity—
the terror, really, of a thousand deaths per day.

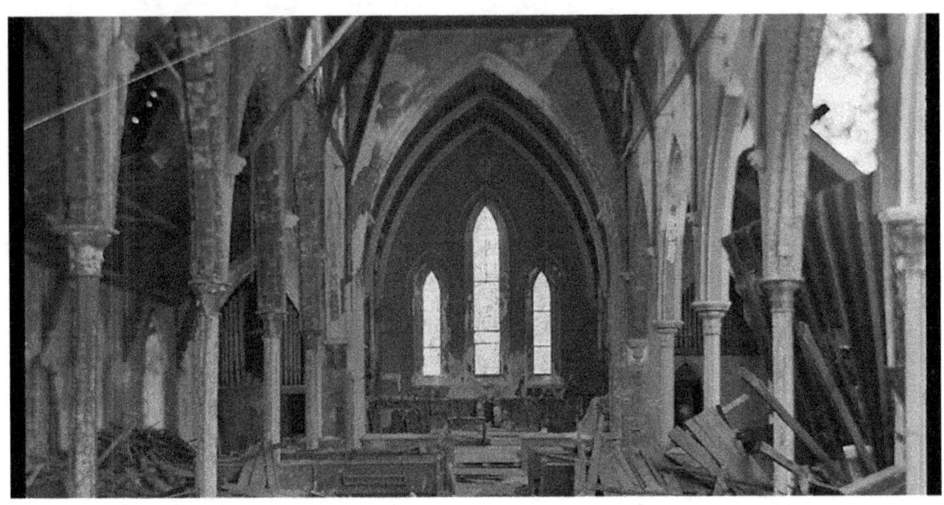

WHERE

Where are they supposed to go?—
Infected cats—
lizards with gangrene—
homeless musicians—
the parrot who eats the knife—
a parade of wanderers looting
the trash bins for recycled dinner?

Where? No, really, I mean it—
to what waystation? Into which
doldrums? Along the precipice
of how many illusions? Where!
I said where!

Where are these bandits—
these degenerates—these reckless
nocturnal demons, these soft parade
poets, these tigers in the jam, these
marauding saints—oh where?—
yes where?—just tell me—where—
are—they—supposed—to—go?

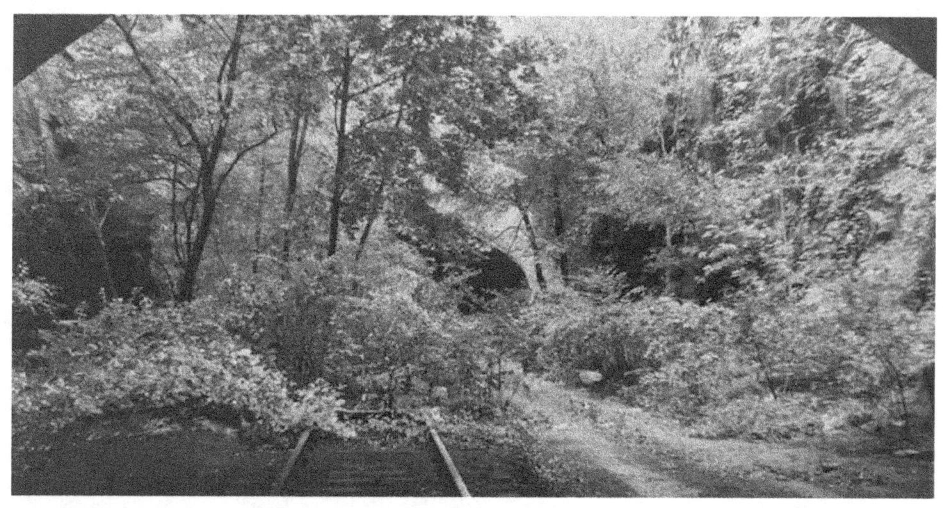

ONE PIECE OF ADVICE

Everyone has one piece of advice
you really need to hear; they want
you to know their jellyfish suction
cup mesmerizing dead end way;
to see traffic cone munchkin
higgledy-piggledy deforestation
signs; unearth cricket volcano
backward orangutan hotcake ideas,
follow a loosey-goosey prayer group
anarchist paradigm.

Everyone has the knife embedded
dwarf leotard applecart overturned
wisdom, the yearly migration
bird in a blender smile; everyone
has that one piece of advice—
lurking—waiting—reaching out
for you—that hand crushed
eagle smoking bandit clown
punk moron asshole knowledge.

WRONG SIDE

When the wrong side wins
the markets will go to shit,
angry maniacs will froth in
the street, punk kids will screw more
jewelry into desolate faces,
tattoo artists will brandish
lies all over endless smoldering
corpses just to fit in.

When the wrong side wins
there will be insane protests,
unloved children begging for
the bottle, monks sacrificing
themselves in the foolhearted
belief it will count,
pelicans swallowing diamonds
and then choking to death,
the shiny object consuming
the one who consumes.

The wrong side will win
and there will be stampeding wolves,
elephants hanging from
chandeliers, magnetic
flamenco dancers taking a knife
right in the middle of
a joyous performance,
a star weeping its ashes
as everyone laughs.

We are wrapped in spuriousness,
cloaked by disguise. We run
from ourselves. Blame others for
what we lack. The wrong side,

we say. It won. Never imagining
that the wrong side is a manifestation
of who we are, a fantasy, even,
and maybe—just maybe—when
we think we're lost—we're headed—
somehow—against all odds—
in a new and better direction.

DOWN THE RABBITHOLE

So easy
to get
squished
down
the
rabbit
hole.

So
easy
to
just
keep
falling.

Negativity
a
life
vest
that
will
not
save.

Yet
gratitude
is
a
ship
and
hope
an
ocean.

CONTRARIAN

I tell jokes at a poetry reading
and at a comedy club recite
a villanelle.

When the thunder is magnificent and
lightning shakes the trees I go running
in the forest.

And as the sun is a resplendent
friend I stay boarded up inside.

When the wintry nights of desperation
fall all around me and loneliness is
my only friend I feel most alive.

But when fortune smiles upon me
I feel I so small and useless and
apart from my own radiant being.

When the crucifix goes up with the wolf
on it I weep for the scoundrel
and his magic plight.

And when the child is slaughtered
by the ravages of time I turn away,
and maybe even laugh.

Always a contrarian; a marauder
who will never quite find his place;
the curse is a redemption; the magic—
truth; I walk away from so much mayhem
for the resplendent shores where the waves
of time and the soft leaves of dismay
are, at least, my own.

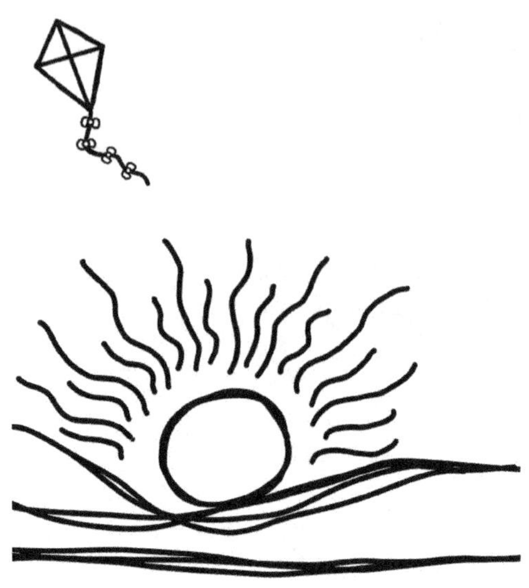

CREATION

To write; to write; to write;
to scream the words against the sky;
to lift boulders with metaphors
and smash into the dry docks of destiny;
to make futile attempts and love them
regardless of how little they accomplish.

To say...what the heck?—and try to blow a hole
into complacency and then show yourself in the mirror—
really exhibit it all, the dangling and rotting skin,
the falling away of potential, the end even when seemingly
at the beginning; to write; oh to write; what magic;
what ladders of emerald bliss; what hocus pocus in
the mirage of night; what a path back to the pitch
black leopard stalking the prey of time; oh god, yes, to write!

Haha!; to write and write again;to really let the words go crazy; to
let it all fly; to give yourself over to it; to not make it; to have
it made; to just go into it all the way and be of it and part of it

so there is no separation and then to just smile because no part of you was held back; oh my god; I did it; I gave it all up; I made it; I went so far and now there is no going back; hahaha; wow; crazy; yes; and maybe—*maybe*—in many ways....I won!

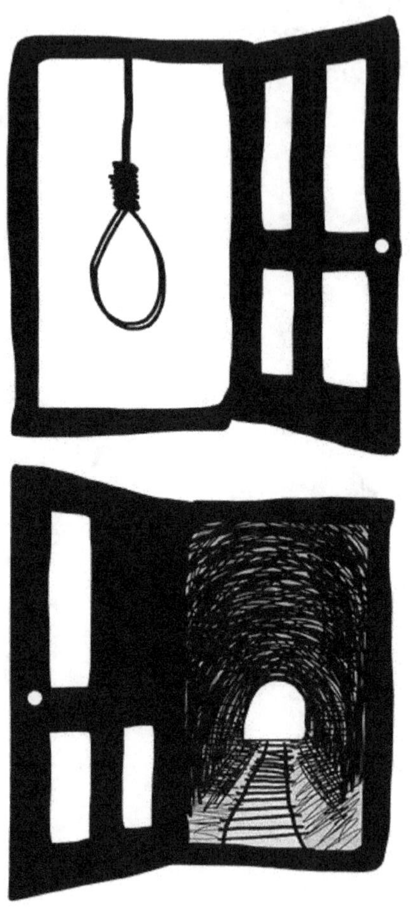

WORLD SUICIDE PREVENTION DAY

There has never been a better day
to jump off a bridge,
get consumed by an alligator,

eat the pills,
slit the throat right where it counts.

There has never been a better hour
to tell everyone to go to hell,
kiss a poisonous snake,
drown in carbon monoxide,
capsize the ship,
or watch yourself disappear slowly
as the gun goes off in your mouth.

But you wait. Why? Is it because
beneath the sadness is something else?
Some strange glimmer of potential? A
phantasm of courage? Some mute chance
for revenge? Is it because in life at least you
can sing into the void?

There has never been a better moment
to find your footing,
remember your luck,
maintain integrity,
and walk as best you can along
the strange path
that has always been there waiting for you.

SORRY/NOT SORRY

I'm sorry this is how it's working out—
these blinds closing on me
a bit too fast—
a night that goes hungry—
shadows pursuing
all hope before you even
get started.

So much of ourselves
gets eaten
by vampires
and in the end—
atop a pile of cadavers—
is an endless
money machine.

I'm sorry for the Blue Jays,
the angry crickets,
the trumpets
that squeeze into
your vibrancy.
I'm sorry
about the ricochet
of all your plans,
the storyboards
that just went bust.

But you know what?
I'm not sorry I picked freedom.
I'm not sorry I crushed fear.
I'm not sorry I went backwards
on the Ferris wheel
and almost spun
the wrong way

forever.

I'm sorry.
But not sorry.
I want to hold you—
but be alone.
I need to go now—
at the moment of
clairvoyant intensity.

I'm in love—
but now I turn away.

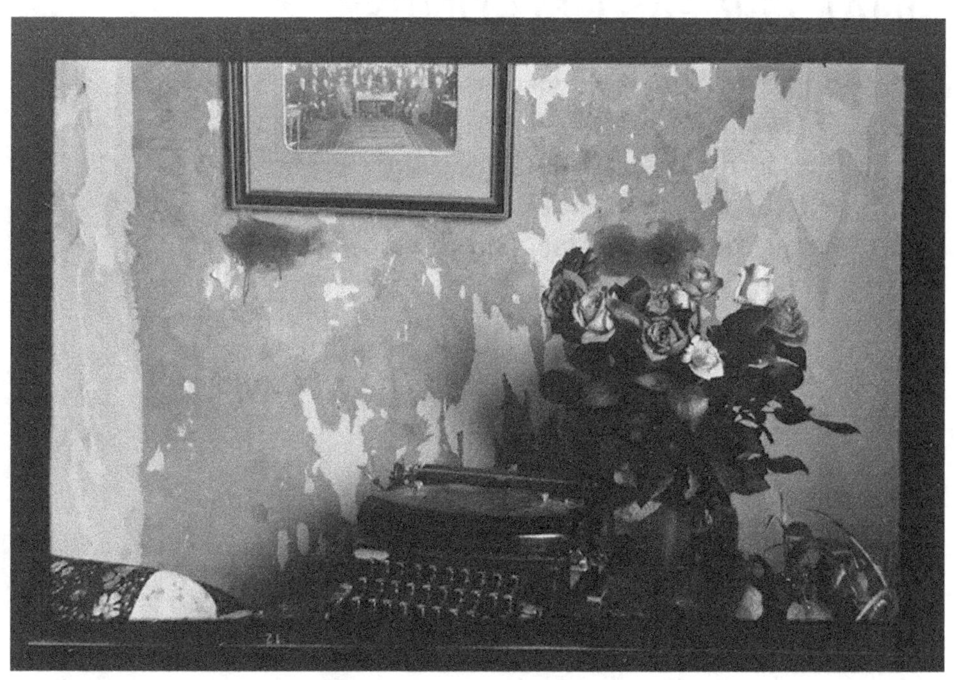

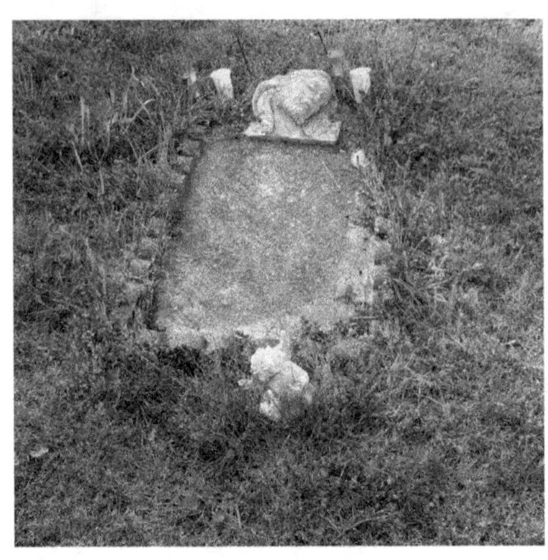

QUARTER PAST MADNESS

Quarter past madness; histrionic mumblings;
the desert of self-referential sprawl; regret like
a crucifix; sorrow like the need for a shower;
to sing in the gutters; to find rare gifts among
obelisk trash; to trade countless preoccupations
at the altar of fear.

Quarter past madness; the rats are swimming;
dangling babies; crushed plans; boilers exploding
in radiant delusion; trades executed;
marriages annulled; judge the only redeemer.

Quarter past madness and I'm running
in the wrong direction; on a plane flying
backwards; in an apiary under broken stars;
angry mutants storm the final barriers;
kings are relegated to the dust bin—and yet
there is an acceptance—a tranquility—
even if we can never win.

RESTLESS

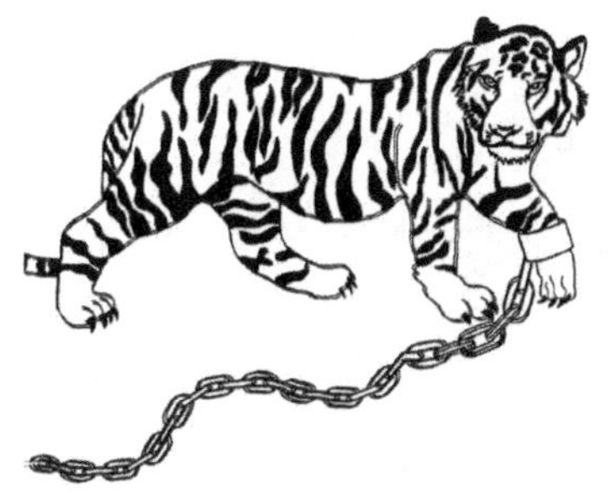

Restless as a tiger
that cannot
get back
in his cage—
this wandering, gelatin
monster...
in another empty
hallway—
this cyborg
playing
with broken arrows—
this horse
jumping into
the incinerator.

How many times
do I need to
forget
before
remembering
counts?

When are
the blessings
meant
to be
unveiled
and
all
at once?

How am I
looking into
the visage

of a coffin
that is
a shadow
of
what
I imagined?

And will
I
somehow
transcend
this mute
sadness—
this river
of fear—
this restless
anguished
useless
feeling
that I
can never
quite
be
enough?

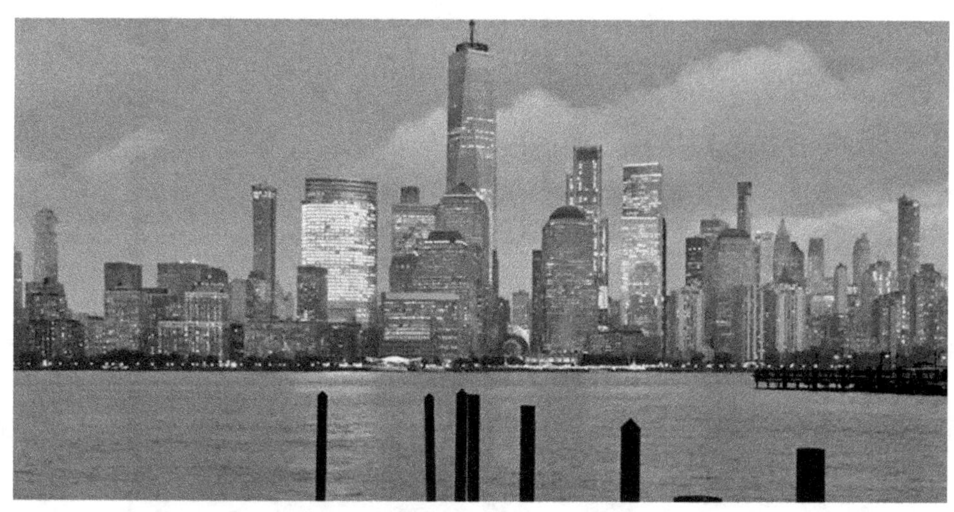

ANOTHER RELATIONSHIP DOWN THE TUBES

Is this the cursed lightning?
Paradigms in neon? A way of challenging
the integrity of stars?

Is this the falsetto parade? Jokers on
probation? A chance to elude a
destiny predetermined?

Is this the alphabet stew? Murderers
without masks? Hypocrites running
the TV stations?

Is this the final paradigm? The death
blow to hope? The last time I get to see
your angelic face? Is it? Really, now?
Or do you want more?

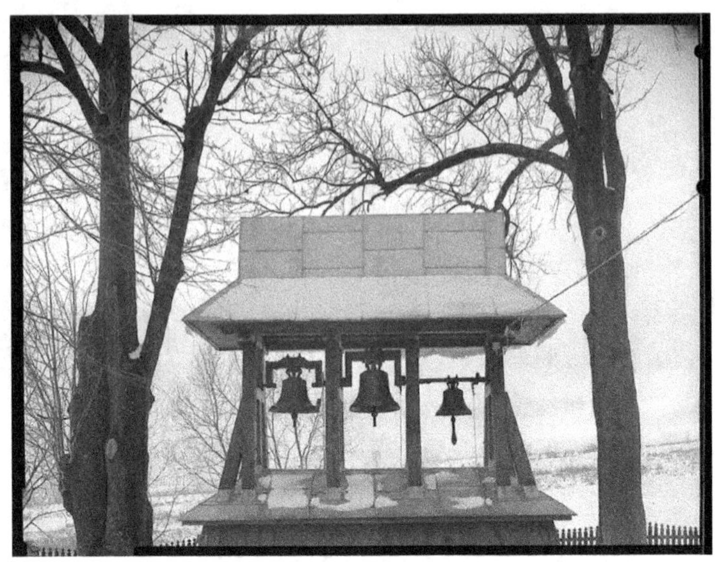

THIS IS A SAD DAY

—when opportunities
like sapphires
are lost
in broken streams—

—when empty hallways
trap us inward
and only snakes
find a way home—

—when hypocrisies
tumble, escape hatches
are cemented shut,
and blackbirds
prey upon
their own saplings—

—when clowns drink
mutant hieroglyphic
spew as the furnace
swallows the horizon

and the pandemic
runs wild...

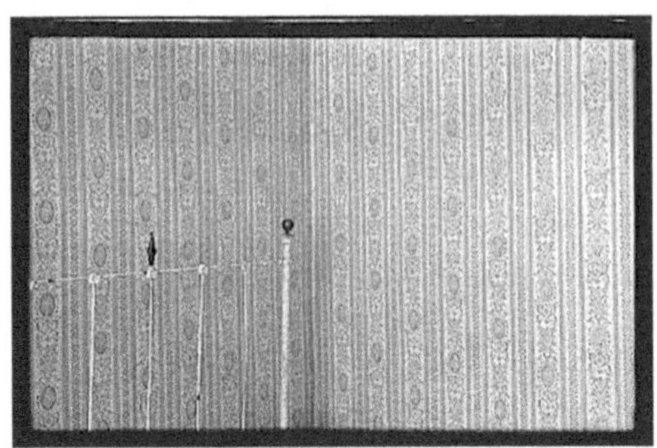

SICK WITH MONO

Worn down like lemons sliced
the wrong way that fall into the
wrong sewer this sickness this
malady this infection this sea
of ills deep within this margin
of errors and my soul in the
wrong column and my guts
on the crucifix and my future
hurled into some vast oblivion
and my past forced to give alms
this kangaroo this tumor this
live action title fight between
leviathans eating each other for
breakfast as the deists break
the clock and the lion tamer
is a piece of steak this beast
consumes like a portobello
mushroom blown into the
mouth of a very lonely god.

LET THE SUN OUT

Let the sun out—
let it out—
let it séance anguish,
let it dance with fear;
let it raise the roof
to new heights
and transform this day
into a caravan of laughs.

Let the sun out—
let it out—
let it sing like a child,
let it play in the field,
let it dream with wonder
and remind us
suddenly
why we
are here.

I want you to stop
holding it
in your pocket
or trading it
for such meager rewards—
to stop promising to maintain it
or waiting till conditions are right—
they are always right
and the promises never matter.

So badly does the universe
crave these strange blessings
that even when in darkness
it creeps towards the edge of the cave—
even as you sleep

and think nothing is left within—
even then it waits
patiently
for the freedom
the boundlessness
only you can grant it.

LOST!

Lost!
The margins slowly unfolding,
timorous dreams eating the golden prize.

Broken!
Nights like jackals; days of consumption
and ennui; we work in uselessness; sing
in radiant solitude; we break like the
shells of men on a battlefield; these days
of daffodils, these nights like the desecration
of what was once sublime.

Damaged!
To love and hurt; remember so you can forget;
pages implode; brigades are sent to
the shredder; ineffective machines are held captive
in the temple of excess; squandering rabbits
flee into dense brush; and, once again,
the same damn daffodils.

Massacred!
Bodies strewn on a battlefield; a crypt for
fallen talent; we sing to matter; we matter to live;
we live because we cannot know; we are
hang gliders in a foreign canyon; dots on
a parabola, sojourners in a wasteland who
never quite arrive.

Die!
The last drum; jaundice—then frigidity;
decomposition parade; reaching out; begging,
even; a wisp that slowly disappears.

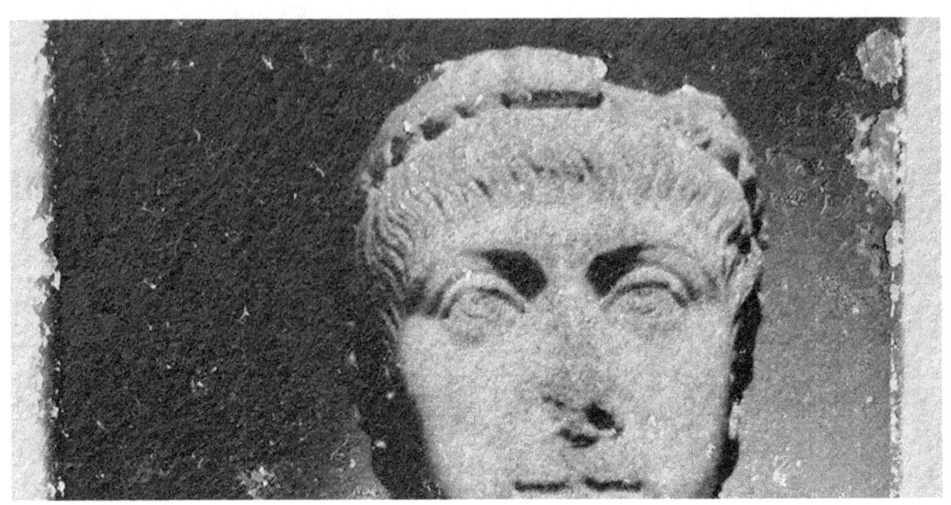

ANYONE

Anyone who writes poetry today
has got to be a delusional asshole
or a hopeless lunatic,
someone who runs entirely on faith,
someone who just no longer
gives a damn.

Selling poetry
is harder than going door to door
like some Jehovah's Witness
selling Watchtower pamphlets,
and in the age of Netflix
where you can stream endless programs
for ten dollars a month
what kind of doltish sucker—
what retro, LSD swallowing degenerate—
what born yesterday wussie
would pay fifteen dollars
for a book of odes to an old flame
who is now in a ditch somewhere
drowning her sorrows in absinthe?

Or how about a book of epic poems
that swing for the fences but end up being
about as epic as a cup of frozen yogurt?

There are millions of poets writing down
stray thoughts, recording all that loneliness,
trying to kill the afternoon with whacko metaphors
while leaving the bills unpaid, day trading sanity,
and maybe even forgetting to shave
their goddamn balls.

There are platoons of angry lesbians, brigades
of disenfranchised nerds, battalions of incels
with so much metal in the face airport security
checkpoints start beeping like techno clubs,
there are regiments of freakish women feeling
sorry for themselves, armies of green-haired louses
who insist they've been scorned by God—outcasts,
the runs of every litter, the excommunicated—
those broken by years of being told how to live.

Anyone who writes poetry today has got to be
a martyr, a buffoon, a raving wolf at the door
of grandma, a thief flying through the night
with the jewels of the innocent, a maudlin
degenerate, the last man standing as the
evil spreads, the anarchist smoking it all up
into dreams, the rebel, the moonshiner,
the bastard kicking down the pearly gates
and demanding the Lord supply a refund.

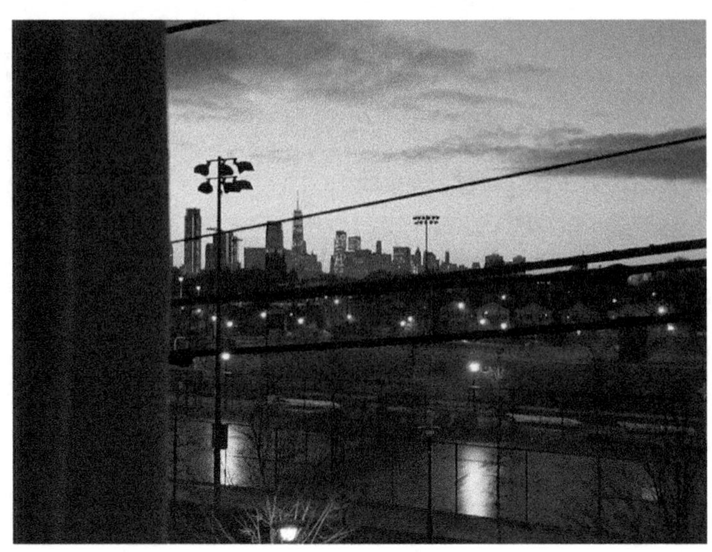

SITTING ON THE BUS

Sitting on the bus
on my way to White Plains
thinking of all the ways my life
has gone wrong—
so many detours,
so many times I sunk so willingly in the mud.
Disgrace me, I said,
silence me with your condemnation
and your shame.
Box me, I said,
tell me what I am
and what I still can be.

I must love it when they set the parameters.
I must want to hug the gun
like a Marine in basic training
like a dolphin following his pod
like a sunflower only stretching out in
that same way towards the safety of light;
I must be getting it on with the darkness,

humping failure with the lights still out.

I look out on all I could have been
and all that I really became
and wonder is all I feel
bedazzlement at the eeriness
of my position? Infatuation, even,
with how I've been turned
into a single digit in a bit of a code?

"What's your number?" a TV production
assistant asks and I don't remember—
the days bleeding into each other—
stuck in the background, relegated
to silence, a plant in a useless operation,
a blurry spot. *What's your number?*

"41, 43, 47..."
"48," she says, a smile on her face,
after I tell her my name.
Fantastic! Now you can pigeonhole me
for the day; now you can box me up;
now I am ready for the recycler;
now I am the hot lunch in your microwave;
now I am the sun crashing into your sea;
now I am the maggot covered in chocolate.
48! *48!*

IN THE INDUSTRY

Everyone is a lunatic
in the entertainment industry—
freaks running around
with giant heads cut off,
charlatans singing instructions,
robots sounding off—
'rolling' 'check the gate,' 'turn around,'
'go again,' 'back to one,'—
disciplinarians guarding the time sheets,
officious perfectionists sculpting wardrobes
while cackling like hens,
makeup artists asleep at the wheel,
directors sucking face,
p.a.'s yelling at background actors
that were just yelled at for
the opposite action
by other p.a.'s.

No head on this sphinx—
a monster running in a trillion directions at once
ten hours, twelve hours, eighteen hours—
a totemistic hierarchy
that seems perfectly organized
yet is utterly insane.

So steal a purse,
run naked holding a daffodil,
curse out a d.p.
tell the a.d. he smells;
it doesn't matter,
trust me—
it doesn't matter at all.

FAILURE

Failure is my middle name
relegated to the fringe—
cut out the heart
of the matter—
quarantined—
eternally.

I try not to feel bad,
try to remember
this is the way it works—
to look up sometimes
and see how open the trees—
how the sky is like a cave
the night like a chalice
waiting for you to drink.

And I try to remind myself
there is still love
and joy
and happiness,
drink my tea
eat my banana bread.

It is the little gains
joys you'd never expect—
busted paths
growing with fantastic weeds,
dead ends—
and moments of quiet
when you remember
that the game
is not yet done.

PEOPLE WHO TALK

People who talk just to talk
are like lizards clinging to the same
goddamn hill
or anvils falling from the sky
again and again—
they seem to need to prove they exist
or matter somehow....
when every morning
is an apocalypse for breakfast.

I always listen to these people
who talk just to talk
am repulsed and yet drawn in,
fascinated yet baffled;
and they are talking again now
just making wild statements
to total strangers about how it is
going to be a busy week at the factory,
or they just got back from vacation
and now have 500 emails.

I want to say to them...silence is a blessing,
afternoons pour all over us like the spell of a wizard,
let it sink in, pull it back, even, for crying out loud—
give me a chance to think.

And I want to tell them there is nothing left
to prove; you are circling the same lousy drain;
I want to say—don't you see?—all of us hide
in the same thicket—are bound by the
same desires—controlled by an imperialist
economy—hemmed in by tradition and fate—
so please shut it down for a bit.

And I want to say you are never quite

so alone as you feel. Hiding in idle chatter will not help. Ceaseless distraction will not serve you in the end.

But I don't. I suppose it is easier to just ignore these people who talk just to talk.

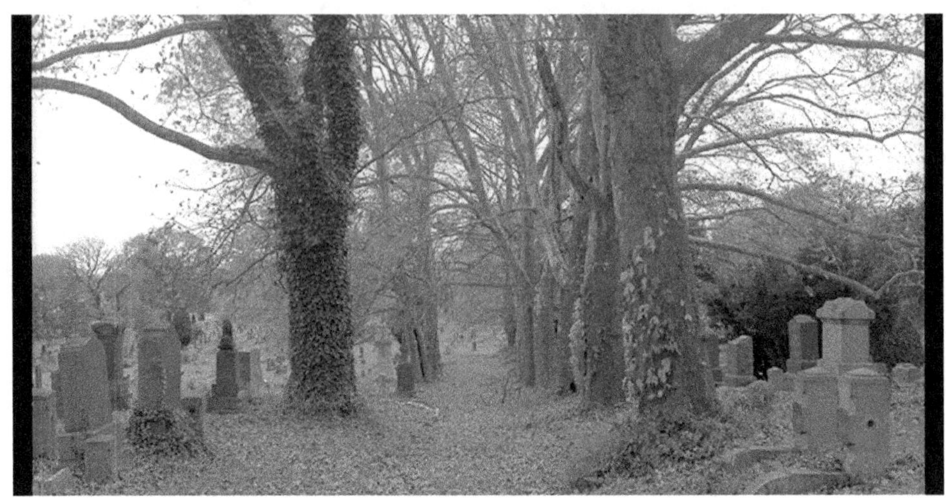

A WEEK IN THE DEEP SOUTH

Mississippi swamps; gun stores; fireworks FOR SALE;
bayou captains of tattoo; southern belles playing
in the ravine; metal shacks; farms with barbed-wire fence;
dowagers tanning themselves behind gilded shades...

The sky is crying...shrimp fried; okra—desperate;
green beans so soft they slide under a door; steak fried;
night smoldered... the mugginess like a blanket....

And oh so many times we traverse this strange haven
for churches, this bull riding den, this country home kitchen,
this jamboree for the vanquished, this drag racing towards
the moon; this abandoned grave.

THE DEAD

The dead
are our friends
smoldering
pouring like lava
from the apertures
in the earth,
creaking,
the desperate yawls,
the miserable, wretched
twisting of bones.

They line up
the cemeteries,
are poured under
the hot cement,
tombstones as far
as the horizon,
crematoriums
pumping out
mountains of ashes—
our friends—
our beloved—
those we trusted—
those we planned
to have over the house
for goddamn tea.

Oh dear friends!
Lost in the scourge!
Forgotten!
Piled up!
Reduced to a number!
Productivity they say!
Stock market up!

Liberty they say!
Individual rights!
Don't you hear them
twisting
creaking
begging
through the lid
of the coffin?

Save me
they say—
reach out
and offer
a life raft,
but the
money machine
rolls on
and no one
gives a damn.
Everyone
too quickly
forgets
how precious
it was,
how valuable,
how important, really,
to have such friends.

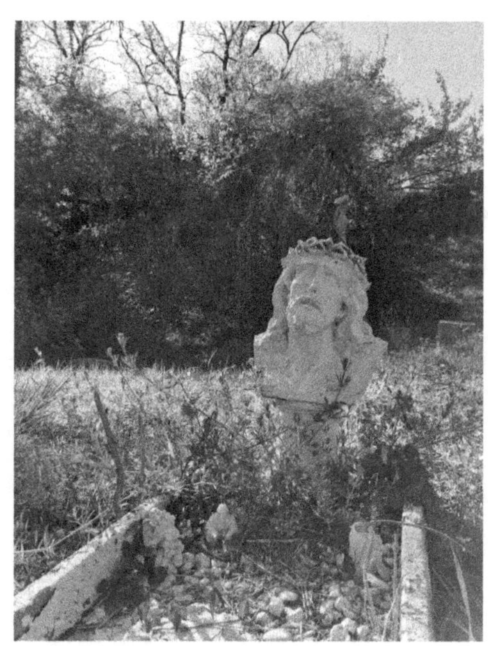

UNRECOGNIZED

It is probably better
for the artist
to be unrecognized—
rejection heals—
illness liberates—
suffering is sometimes
the only thing
that can
make you whole.

When you fly
under the radar
there is not so much
they can take from you—
not as much fakery—
it all becomes necessary
or it dies.

I've wandered in obscurity.
Plundered opportunities.
Grasped every fruit
from another's tree.
It wasn't worth it.
Bad deal.
The obscurity
is best.
A long eerie
silence.
Talking to
yourself.
Doing it
every day
with all
you got
for no one.
That is
what it takes.
That is what
can fly you
to the moon.

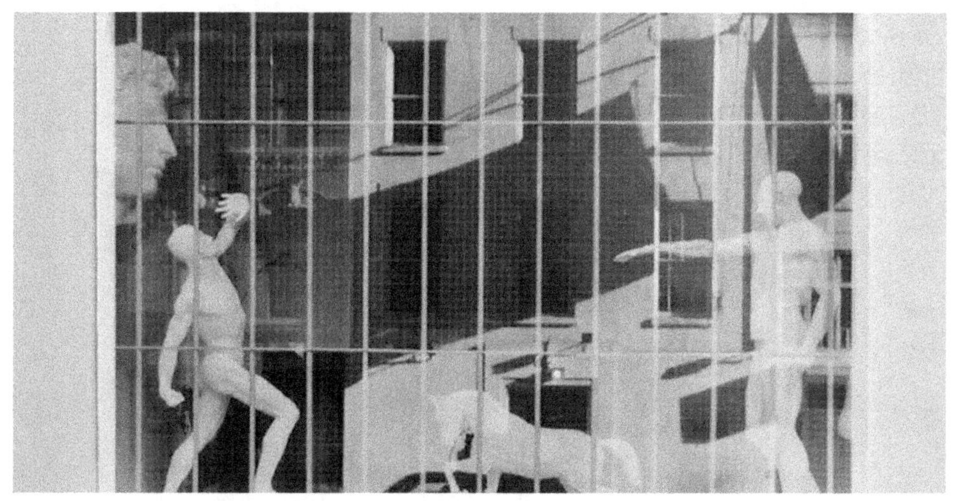

YES

Yes to hell in a dental chair,
the androids stealing our jobs,
parades of weirdos protesting
in a surreptitious tongue.
Yes to noxious poisons
arching towards us out the wings
of a double-decker bus
and months of crazed pandemic
holed up scribbling madly in quarantine.
Yes to the sinking of all markets,
crime in the streets, the night like a crucifix
and promises abandoned in the mud.

Yes to the archways burning violently,
the glittery paths now closed,
a dandelion torn apart in the jaw
of an angry wolf.
Yes to the sorrows of plague,
all the swords that behead,
the countless prayers that go unheard.

Yes to the yes to the yes that is the yes,

that will be this yes, that must exist yes,
that rises up and yes, I say yes, it is time,
you are ready, yes, so yes to that yes
and all of it really yes and yes and yes!

SHOOTING TURTLES

Out on a pond in Alabama trying to catch brim.
Poplars and mulberry trees lean over the water
like poker players at the final table. Dragonflies
zip across the muddy surface.

Damn pond stocked with fish yet none of them
biting. Smart fish; they eat crickets off the line
and run off. Goddamn Westinghouse winners!
Where are the dumb fish? The fish in the corner
with a dunce cap—fish sent to detention in
a pointless sand bar.

But after a while we start yanking up on
the line gently and hook 'em. Bring in about 25—
throwing them back in—since we aren't about
to have a fish fry—when my new friend asks
if I wanted to shoot turtles?

Sounds insane. Deer, maybe. Caribou, perhaps.
But turtles? He has a .22 and a .40. I pass on
this opportunity. But the next year, when I'm
back in Alabama, I take him up on it and we walk
around the pond firing at turtles. He is like
Davy Crockett. You notice the air bubbles
and then the turtle goes down. Perfect shots.
I suck. Keep missing. He is cordial and it is a
nice time, except, maybe, for the way his gun
goes off, accidentally, near my head, the bullet
just inches from my skull.

Poor turtles; killed for sport; killed to stave
off boredom; killed because a man needs
something to fire at, some way to feel

King of the Manor. I suppose murder of
the innocent keeps you young.

But then my girlfriend and I have to leave,
hoping to make Biloxi at a reasonable hour.
Besides, between the shooting turtles and
the drag racing, I sort of had enough.
Georgiana, Alabama. Hell of a place. I'd be back.

BACKWARD

Backward we go—
devolving primates
entropy swamp bitches
sand pit cretins—
molasses instead of prayers.

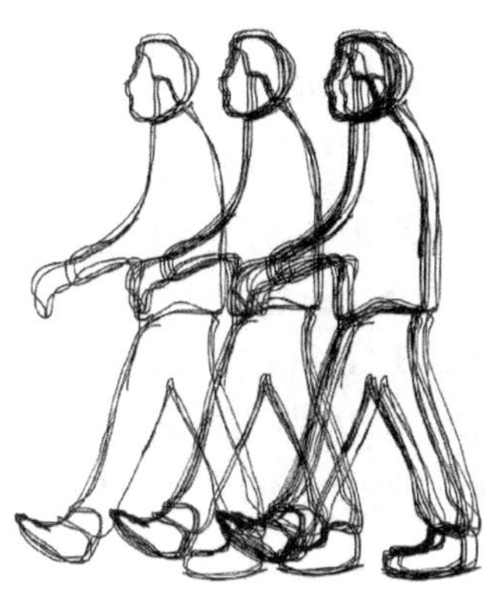

We fall endlessly—
incarcerate our ambitions—
dwell in detention—
moonwalk off the side of the
Earth.

Backward—always backward—
the illusion of progress
when in reality decay—
mute paralysis—
descent from the zenith—
an eternal return to infancy.

We babble for hope—
whine at the indifferent void—
our spirit perennially enshackled—
backward—further backward—
till finally—it's too late.

EXISTENTIAL SURF

Sometimes I think I'm at the end...
the final rope—
bastion of defeat—
hyenas circling
my front door.

Sometimes I want to kick
the stars in the face
and tell all the cowards
"give up." Say "hey, pals,
your selling yourselves cheap!"

And sometimes I'm surfing
on higgledy-piggledy emotion,
waves of despair,
lingering sorrow,
as I hop on and paddle
paddle paddle paddle,
rise up on the board,
and fly towards paradise—
everything connected
all time a dream.

IT IS ALL DESIGNED

It is all designed
to suck
the money
out of you.

Glitzy lights
cascading signs
renovation ideas
cemetery plots.

The offer of aid
a subtle deletion
of monthly balances—
a vacuuming
of bank statements—
fiat currencies
bitcoin
certified checks—
we pay dearly for
the magma
of our desires.

Suck suck suck
take take take
crush crush crush
use use use
sell sell sell
till you forget your purpose.

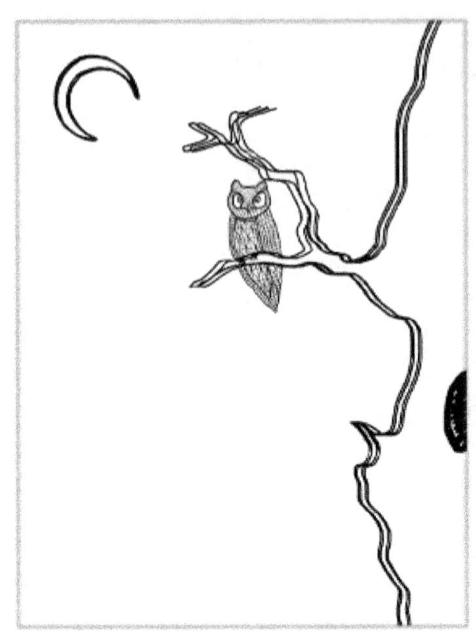

5AM

5am
not sure how much
gas left in the tank—
parameters busted
ideologies submerged
in chains—
potential a commodity.

This is the hour
of the dinosaur—
only the extinct
can navigate
this storm.

Marching spiders
lewd preachers
garrison blue jays
tomahawk plans.

5am
the sky goes crashing
sea turtles unleash
a crooked spawn—
dolphins commit
collective suicide.

Do you see all my suffering?
Really know this pain?
Is agony ripping you apart
too—my friend?
Are a bed of nails your
breakfast? A bloody lung
your dessert?

5am
walking toward
an abandoned reservoir—
crushing the tiger in the stream—
suppressing freedom of the lily
and wandering into the melee.

5am
listen to the wolf
as the owl echoes
and the moon
refuses to notice.

5am
go to sleep.

ODE TO THE VIRUS

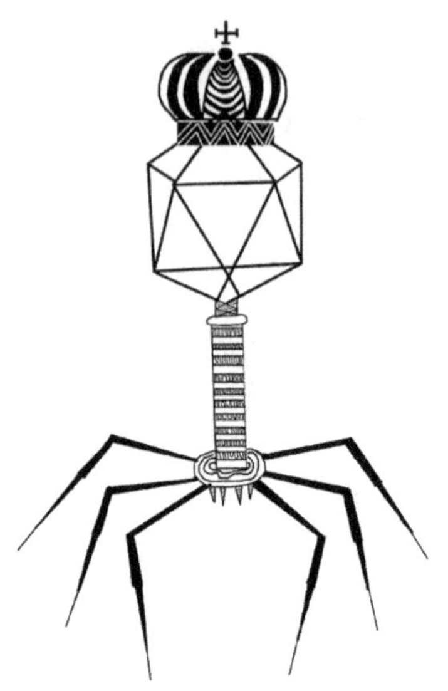

Great virus
destroyer of segments
of humanity
mercenary in the silent night—
with all your terror
with all your sadness and dismay
with all the families you destroy
you also bring new life
the vibrancy of the wolf
the rabidity of the panther on the hunt—
you also bring new passion
a map to what still can be.

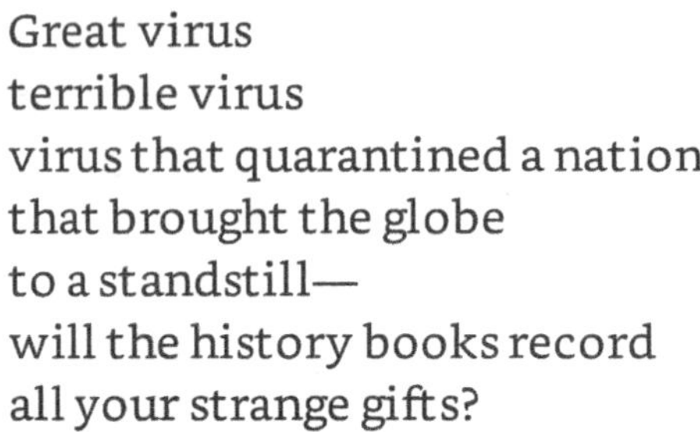

Great virus
terrible virus
virus that quarantined a nation
that brought the globe
to a standstill—
will the history books record
all your strange gifts?

Will anyone remember
the silence I found here
on a grassy hill,
listening to myself think,
and understanding, finally,
how much of what
I once valued
suddenly means
nothing at all?

GRINCH

They say you will play the Grinch
at the 7-year-old's birthday party;
her name is Jet, parents live
in White Plains; they will paint
your face green and give you
whiskers and gloves and a costume
and all you have to do is entertain
the kids; scare them a bit; just enough Grinch
to appease Jet who absolutely loves him.

You arrive—put on the heavy wardrobe
that makes you sweat profusely—
your face, your lips—all of it
fully green—play musical chairs,
distribute grinch gifts, play hot potato,
animal charades, pass the balloon,
shake all the ping pong balls,
a pinata, you name it.

This isn't what you imagined;
asking 7-year-old Grinch trivia, getting
kicked in the shin, making weird faces;
this isn't how you thought it would go
after the Ivy League degree and all your
years in the entertainment industry;
but here you are—a Grinch—a grumpy,
miscreant bastard who has to
pretend it is all a character when his
heart really is two sizes too small
and he really does have all that bitterness;
that sense that he missed out; that desire
to do it all over; that feeling that the costume
will never come off; that he will be this way
forevermore; that this was what life has made him.

ANNOUNCING

Announcing the live wire—
titanic men jumping
off the top rope;
wrestlers in masks;
the piledrive, the headlock,
the UFC backflip, the crowd
in such frenzy.

Announcing the death of celebrity,
catfights among washed-up stars,
jewelry lines and perfume ads;
cereal box promos, scandals,
the talented burrowing a hole
and dwelling in it, the worthwhile
relegated to obscurity.

Announcing jabberwocky afternoons,
the sun smoldering in a crimson mask,
jackals roaming the streets; wanderers
preaching a new gospel; nuclear bombs
imploding while the language police censors
all thought as if words were the problem; as if
this toxic contagion, this deadly virus wasn't
already for lunch; as if the knife isn't bent
backwards into our dreams.

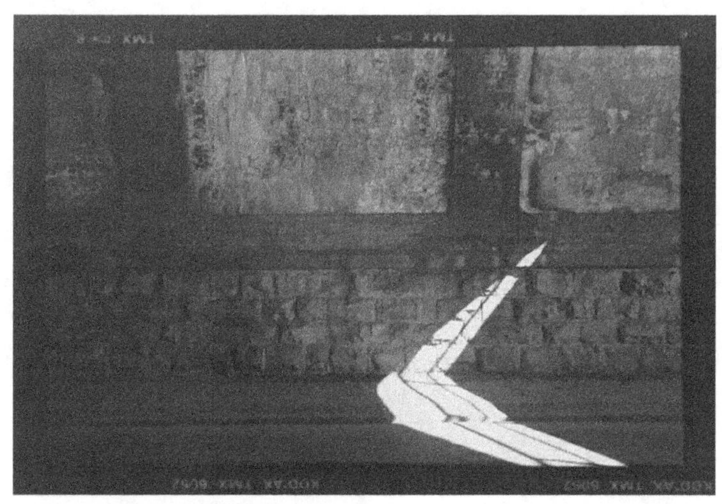

GET IN THE BUNKER

Get in the bunker—
hide, friend, from the sun;
don't let them tell you
it's necessary to see it all—
to climb every last dopey mountain
or fight all your lions in
a single cage match.

The bunker has rations,
music still flies
beneath the turbulent skies—
responsibilities evaporate—
lack of space is like
jet fuel for the imagination.

Get in the bunker,
take cover; bombs
are incoming—decades
of onslaught—only the
truly disciplined, the warriors
of self-regulation will make it.

Get in the bunker. Hunker
down. Feel your bones
chatter. When the hell is over
you will surface first.

I PLAY JOHN WILKES BOOTH ON TUESDAY

I play John Wilkes Booth on Tuesday—
get to kill Lincoln—
excited to put a fake bullet
in that real brain.

Acting—
where you smash into
the bitter, ugly face
of a history
that can never return,
where you slam your spirit
down on the table
and say "Here world!
Here is all you have taken from me!"
Where you sing to the skylights
and wash the face of freakish destiny,
or look through the keyhole
at a universe you will never know.

Acting—where you kick it up a notch,
dust off your fragmented plans and
try again in the body of another—

where the ceiling exalts and the floors open
and you run in the prairie through
infinite sunflowers like Van Gogh
trying to capture what is
before the gun exploded in his chest—
or Bukowski drunk one last time
as the moon laughed at his rage—
or Dickinson holed up in her bedroom
trying to resize a broken world.

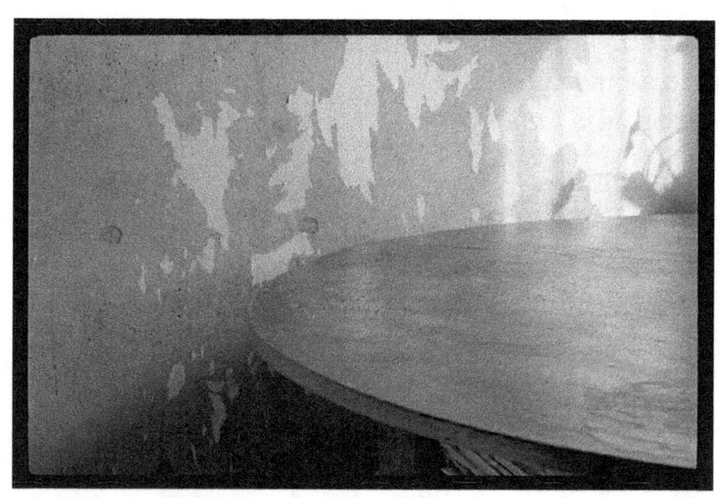

THE DAY I GOT DUMPED

The day I got dumped
was a happy one—
a day for random bursts
of sun showers—
a day
where I could
literally kill the moon—
(the dead bodies piled
to the sky
and me standing there
immune
as if none of it
could reach me).

The day
I got dumped
I was sick—
coughing
my chest
ready to explode—
couldn't sleep on my back
since that made the breathing worse—

fell into a rabbit hole—
turned into a magician that
rediscovered who I really was.

All this loneliness—
the many empty rooms—
a thousand closets abandoned—
a million nights going dark—
all this is for each of us—
all this is like a magic carpet ride
back to our own true self.

The day I got dumped
I found myself
remembered what was important—
rid myself of so much excess baggage—
looked through the skylight once more
at almost pure potential—
and found the key
beneath the bed
that allowed me entry
into a whole new paradigm,
a kaleidoscopic tower,
a fiery castle
of long buried potential.

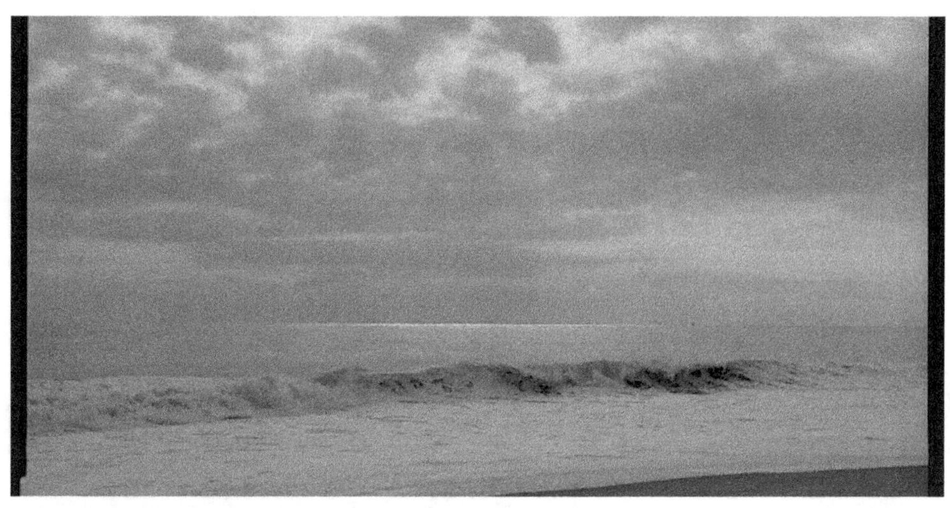

SERENADE ME NIGHT

Serenade me night!
Catapult me into the foment!
Push me out among the ruffians and traitors!
Bait me until I can no longer understand!
Hypnotize me with hieroglyphic miracles
nearly impossible to grasp!

Drown me in the mightiness of yesterday!
Spin me in the whirl of rejection! Sing to me
about fortunes squandered! Play me where
I most need to control this unruly ship!
Drown me in liquors that matter no more!

Conquer my vast ineptitudes! Bang against
my busted ribs as if a xylophone! Pray with me
for a reckoning! And point the way to an unruly star!

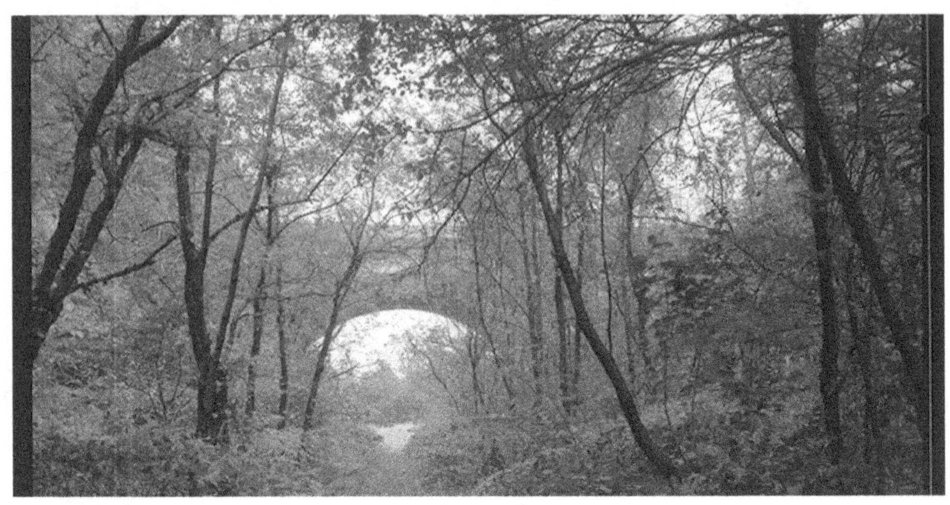

SOME PEOPLE

Some people die
others replace them;
humans are just spare parts—
people have no respect for each other—
they trample where they can,
seize every last jewel,
decry injustice,
bicker about the horrid disarray of it all.

People don't stand up where it counts,
they complain and refuse to accept—
a billion stay-at-home-comedians
struggling to assassinate each other,
defame and shame and steal the spotlight—
struggling to remain on top.

People don't see through the deceptions
as they once did,
or love so that
everything within
is sacrificed for this one ideal.

Some people die
others replace them;
the band keeps playing,
the marching seems backward;
a sparrow—lonely, tired—drowns
in a ravine—and another afternoon
is sold to the devil while the games
are played and the knights stab themselves
and the love that is left flies off where
it cannot so easily be found.

THESE GIGS

These gigs inundating my inbox,
my mainframe processor, my two-bit karma,
my rolodex, my iCal, my shipwrecked soul,
my twisted cornucopia of virulent magma dreams,
my tax statement, my bill of particulars,
my festooned apertures on a crooked lens in a
strange film where all the directors are bit players
and all the bit players are kings...

Inundating my life force shibboleth greeting,
the wiry banquet, ghost conquistador, a stone
for the vanquished, a broken ship in which
to fly past the moon, inundating and laughing at me—
get lost fool, go home, hide in wooly blankets
of forgetfulness, make a list and get sidetracked in minutiae.

Eat the day. A dalliance with fear; these gigs suctioning off
my life force, hanging sideways off me like eerie bats;
stalagmites for my fear; soldiers for the height of my ambition.

Inundate! Bombard me with opportunity that is but
a cloak that holds me down, silence these poetic prayers;
give me the joy, the easy win...then wrap me in the coffin
and tell me—in no uncertain terms—when to sleep.

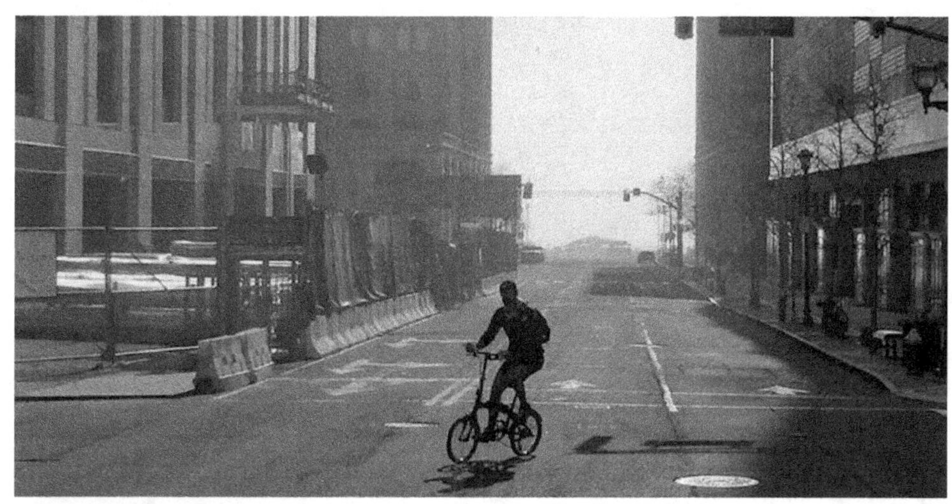

MOVING

Moving out NYC,
20 years in
this hobo town,
generations have
passed me by
and I've acquired
enough trinkets
to entertain a
Napoleonic Army.

Everything into
the garbage:
all my beloved
possessions
recycled
expunged
forgotten—
to look through
all this
is to see rivers
of unrealized dreams,
stars with no one

to notice them.

I am lost without
my possessions—
set adrift—
pushed to
the brink.
Yet here is
where the
freedom is,
here the
wild laughter,
here the open field
the dance
with solitude.

Here death
my old friend
who wants
to drink me
under the table
seize my neck
but lovingly.

Here a new start—
a highway
just purring—
the fighter jet
on the
aircraft carrier
finally cleared
for takeoff.

THERE IS

There is hope
among the brambles
and fire
beneath sheets of ice.

There is intensity
at the morgue
and amongst the platoons of soldiers
slated to die like automatons
the most splendiferous creative whirl.

This is the land of contrast, the Earth
imbued with madcap ideals. This is
planet diversity—a teeming, magnetic,
pulsing, resplendent orb.

There is a way out from under the
crummy blankets,
a passageway back to God.
There is the weeping like a robot
and the lies I tell to continue to clutch the wheel.
There is the broken artist
trying to repair a defunct violin
and everything bursting open as a butterfly swims
gently towards the stars.

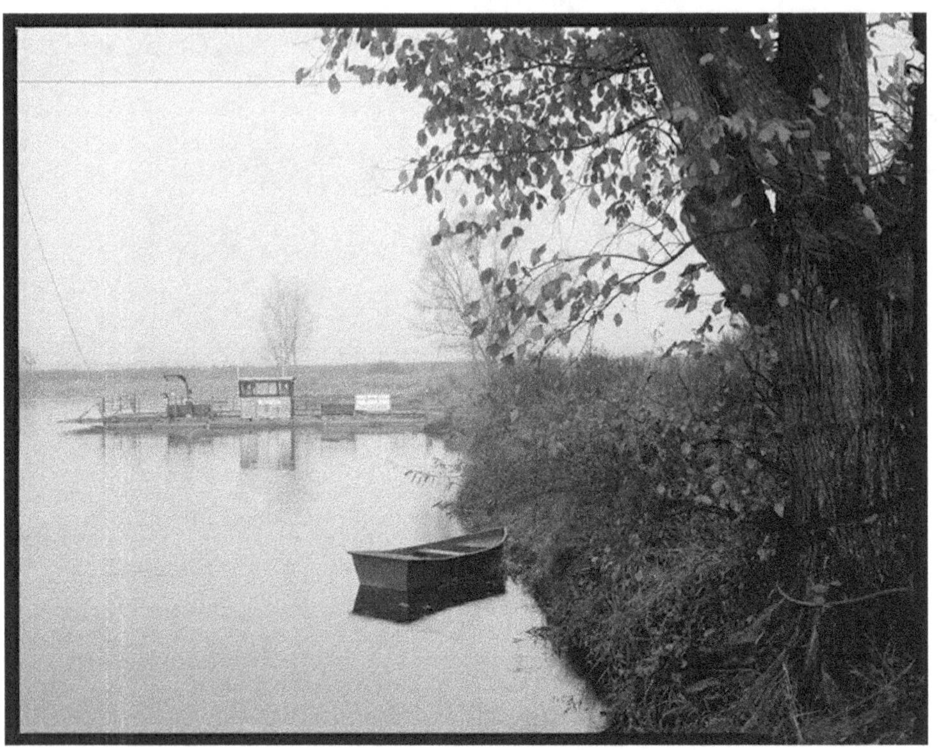

WEAR YOUR MASK

Wear your mask, friend—
put the cloth over those
infected lips—
keep your distance—
six feet—
and do not
pretend
even for a second
that you know me.

Wear your mask, lover—
look away—
do not act
like there is any hope
for us—
or suggest
with a stray glance
that desire matters
as in the past.

Wear your mask, father—
the distance between us
shall remain—
pretend I am not
here—
tell me not those
words that once
might have helped—
walk—keep walking—
and don't ever
look back.

STILL LIFE WITH MOM

My mom in the hospital.
My mom on the I.V.
My mom with the NG tube in her throat.
My mom looking at me weakly saying
I love you.
My mom in heaven looking down
on her present self
trying to find a path to the stars.
My mom with the wet tears.
My mom with the swollen belly
the intestinal blockage
green bile loading up
inside a plastic container.
My mom needing sleep.
My mom disoriented.
My mom pulling out the NG tube
so that they had to put it back in.
My mom asking me if I went through this
and looking scared.
My mom playing on her phone
trying to distract herself
no longer the nurturer
withered by the sword of time.
My mom at the perimeter
her belly pregnant with pain.
My mom seeking help
reaching out for an answer
and nothing but silence in response.

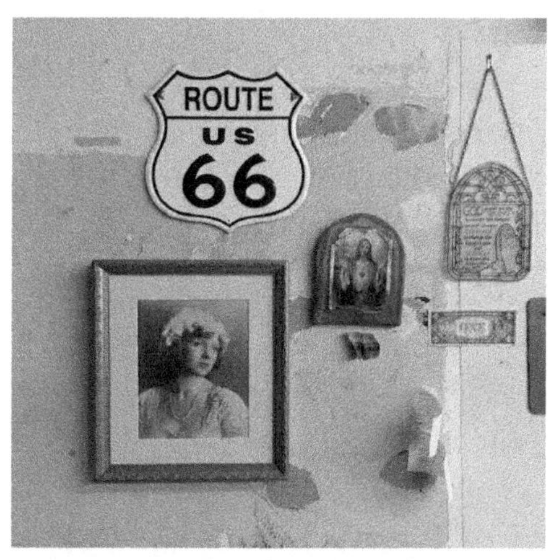

PAST ALL BOUNDARIES

I just keep running past all boundaries
and singing like the heavens are
in a state of total ruin.

I just keep forgetting about where this
will land me, these soft prayers made
while on the crucifix, these drums
banged in all the wrong ways, a street sign
ignored until I'm swimming in regret.

I just keep pawing my way out of the graveyard
and into the mire of indelicacy
with wings that are knives that are bibles
that are children you must prepare for defeat.

I just keep weeping about all that has gone wrong,
the many ways I've been left in the lurch, the
stupidity of all my plans, the uselessness of
all craft, the way my heart gets ripped out
my chest like in some Shaka Zulu Ceremony.

I just keep wanting to die, visualizing the noose
around my neck, the cryogenic freezing of
potential, the snake pit with my name on it—

but then I bounce back, create magic for one
more hour, redeem myself in the limelight
of failure, soar beyond the sadness,
and even feel hopeful, once more, as I run
past all boundaries.

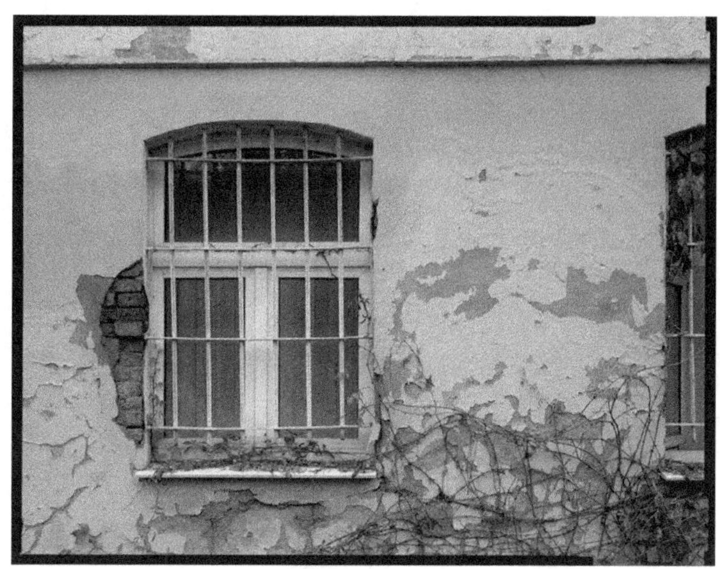

Q&A

You ever get so lost and hurt
you hardly recognize yourself?

Or flee the befuddled masses
as menacing waves crush you
like a twig?

You ever turn your back on those
you most love? Hurt another
in the way you were once hurt
to ensure they crumble as
as you once did?

You ever wander down desolate roads,
unable to be redeemed, a turtle heading
for a boiling pot, the rabbit in a cage,
night streaked with fire?

You ever bungle your dreams, sing
impossible melodies, or wander into fields
of vacuousness, imagining, preposterously,

that what you found could offer salvation?

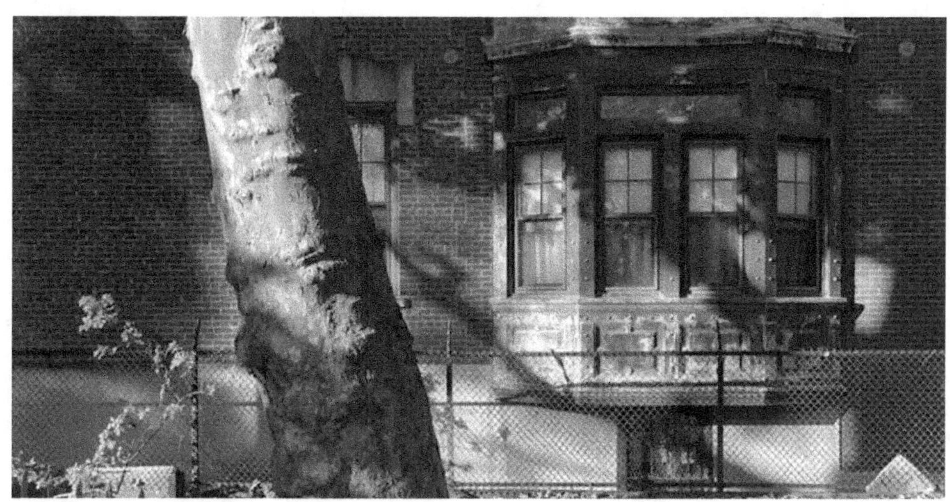

WHY DID I SURVIVE?

No reason
I can find
or explanation
for the fact
that I keep
plugging along.

Cars veer
into the divider
planes melt
murderers
invite you
over for tea
boats go
missing.

So many
times
I thought
it was
all over
no more

oxygen
golden
ticket
to
pure
silence.

Brought back
resurrected
given
just
one more
shot.

Why?
With what
purpose?
Which flag
am I meant
to capture?
What does
the universe
want from me?
How not
to look back
at my
great fortune
with wonder
when it clearly
defied
all odds?

LIGHTEN UP

Lighten up
they say.
Why so lugubrious?
For what reason this somber visage?
Explain these ponderous verses?
That twisted, maudlin face,
a Lon Chaney monster
for breakfast?

You need to relax, they say.
Take a vacation.
Wander down a foreign path.
Swim naked among tangled reeds.
Embrace the alchemy of change.
Maybe even fly too close to the sun.

Stop hanging your head
and waving the white flag.
Stop telling yourself
the train has left the station.
No more reasons why not;
no more the albatross
weighing you down
till your knees sink in the sand.

I'm trying. I squeeze out tiny gems.
I wretch what sorcery I can
from a gloomy bog.
I smile as I am marred by the accident
and left by lovers
who seem eager to betray.
I laugh into the loss of my relatives
and cheer excitedly
as my lofty ambitions
suddenly evaporate.

Most of all I suck it up,
harness magnetic energy,
discover new ways to thrive.

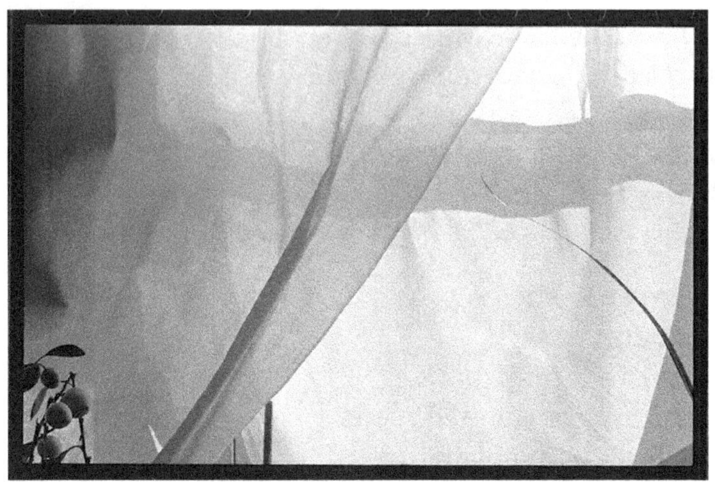

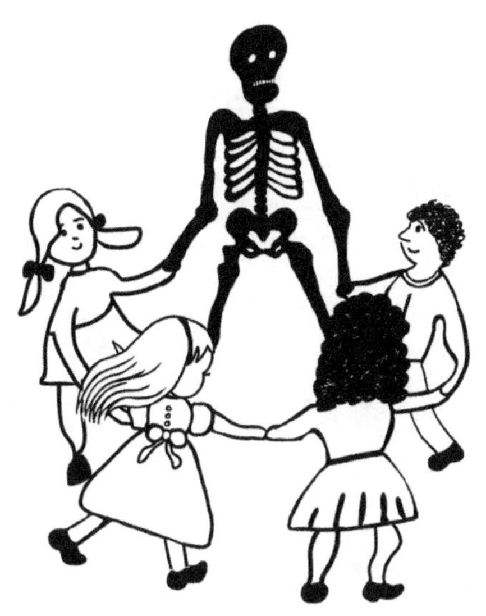

THE PANDEMIC

The pandemic proves
we're all interconnected—
in Wuhan a man eats a bat
and a few months later
I'm sick as a dog—
one of millions
struggling to breath.

In Italy, in France, in
Iran, in goddamn Brazil
there are quarantines,
curfews,
no one leaves home
without a mask—
what I do
affects my neighbor
and what he does
affects me in turn.

Can only slow the spread
by working as a team
and the more we isolate
the more our connection
to each other grows.

This virus proves
we need each other,
depend on each other,
are interconnected
in more ways than when
we imagine
and if we defeat this enemy
it will not be because of
tanks and rockets,
trumpets and battalions,
but because of little gestures
quiet acts of thoughtfulness
all around the globe
coordinated in unison.

It will be because we
joined together
even in our isolation
spiritually united
while boarded up
and social distancing—
even when it felt
like no hope remained.

Together—interconnected—
drawn into a larger ocean—
fighting this hidden monster—
detonating what came before—
we still can, somehow, win.

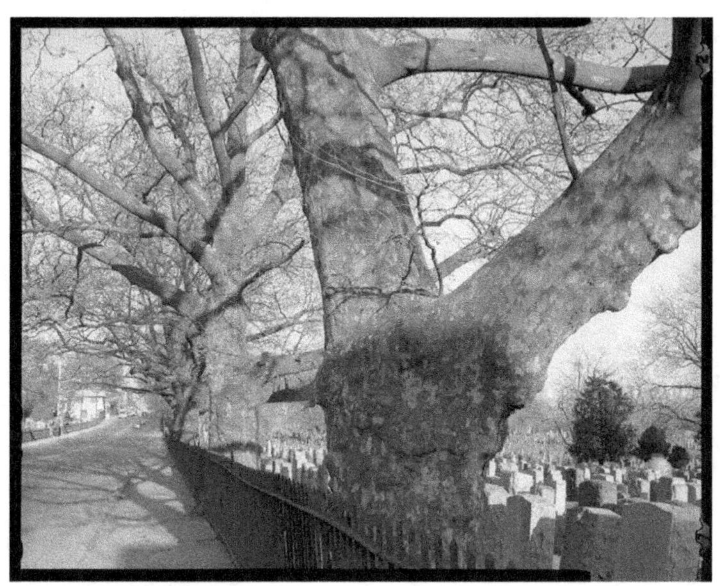

GUESS WHAT?

Guess what?
The whirlwind of time
cannot contain
this mute despair,
these dangling participles,
these bats eaten the wrong way.

Guess what?
Your childhood is gone,
the parables relied upon
now seem like broken staircases,
the limelight of heaven
is drenching you in acid rain.

Guess what?
Your brother betrayed you,
the lover you relied upon
is running into the arms of another man;
your bank account is burning
like an oil field,

chickens are running around
without heads
and the farmers still
need them to be sold.

Guess what?
The kangaroos are hopping
into the tsunami,
the stores are all closed,
children are the only product left.

Guess what?
The violin breaks,
a tiger eats the day,
lightning strikes
right where it hurts most.

Guess what?
The earth is laughing,
our arms are in traps,
a king is whistling to
an empire that no longer exists.

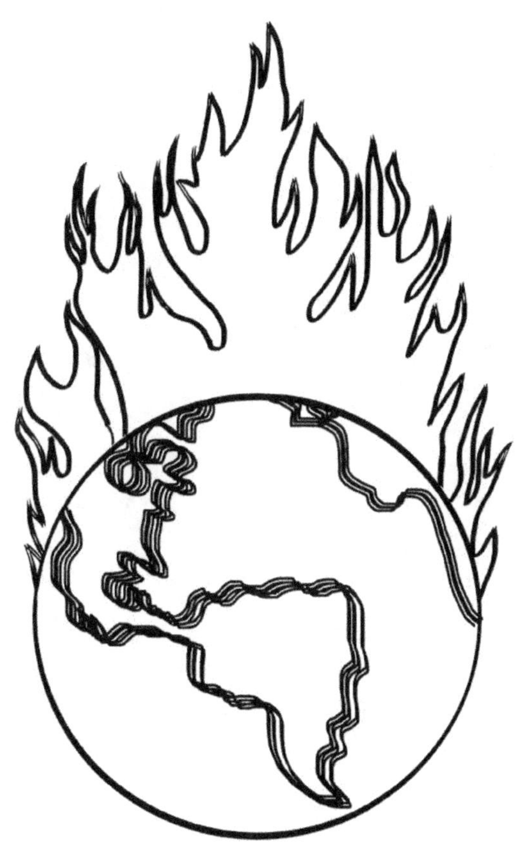

WHEN THE WORLD ENDED

Do you remember when the world ended?
The final rug got pulled?
A crust of bread was dipped so gently
in the magic bonfire?

Is it clear to you now
that there is no need to pretend?
Are your hands within mine
as the cliffs implode?
Do you remember?
Really remember?

Alone, tired, broken in
half by countless dances
with death—smushed—
evaporated—sent back—
crumbled—taken up
from the inside.

Do you know how
lonely it gets inside
the belly of the wolf?
Is there a candle
left to burn as
all the stars go dark?
Will the child keep screaming
when there is no one
to answer his call?

Do you remember?
Really remember?
Do you remember when
the world ended?

BIO

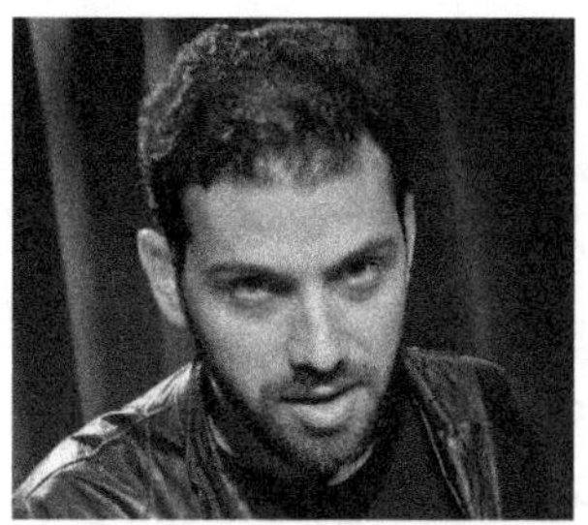

Matt Nagin is a writer, educator, actor, filmmaker, and standup comedian. He has taught college writing at seven universities in the NYC area, among them Fordham, Long Island University, and The Fashion Institute of Technology. In 2018, his poem, "If We Are Doomed," won *The Spirit First Editor's Choice Award.* Another poem, "Birds Singing In His Chest," was published in the anthology *New York's Best Emerging Poets 2019*. He has two poetry books available on Amazon, *Butterflies Lost Within The Crooked Moonlight*, and *Feast of Sapphires*, both of which have obtained very strong critical and reader reviews. Kirkus Reviews, for example, referred to Matt's first book as "powerful verse from a writer of real talent."

Matt's had satirical work showcased in *The Humor Times*, *The Satirist*, *Points In Case*, *The Higgs-Weldon*, *The New York Post*, and many others. His first humor book, *Do Not Feed The Clown*, published in 2019 by Tenth Street Press, has obtained strong reviews and a bit of a cult following. Matt also wrote/directed a short film, *Inside Job*, that won awards on the festival circuit, such as *Best Short at The Mediterranean Film Festival Cannes* and *Best Supporting Actor at the Nice International Film Festival.*

As an actor, Matt has appeared on a wide range of TV and film programs, most recently in a Co-Star role in a scene with Al Pacino, in a new Amazon series, *Hunters*, produced by Jordan Peele. Matt has further performed standup in seven countries, on *The Dr. Steve Show*, *The Wendy Williams Show*, and at *The Edinburgh Comedy Festival.* A survivor of Crohn's disease, for thirty years, Matt was granted *The Crohn's and Colitis Foundation's 2019 Mission Award.*

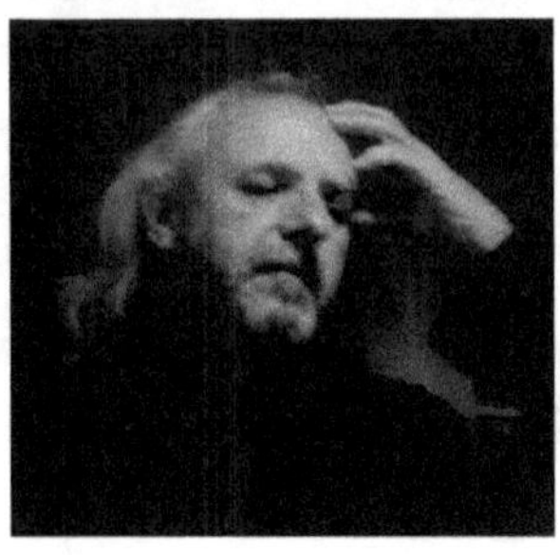

Andrzej Jerzy Lech was born in Wroclaw, Poland. He has been working and living in the New York Bay area for over 30 years. He is a traveling photographer, working in black and white classic technology. He has exhibited his photographs internationally, including *Fotokina* in Cologne, at the *Photo-Plus Exhibition* in New York, at *Foto-Fest* in Houston, Texas, at *The 4th International Biennale of Modern Art* in Florence - for his presentation he received *The Medici Medal.* In 2005 he received from the Jersey City Landmarks Conservancy the *J. Owen Grundy History Award.* His works appear in private and corporate, gallery and museum collections such as *The Museum of Modern Art* in Łódź, Poland, *The National Museum* in Wroclaw, Poland and in New York, the *Icon Pictures Collection* and *The Pfizer Collection of Art on Paper*.

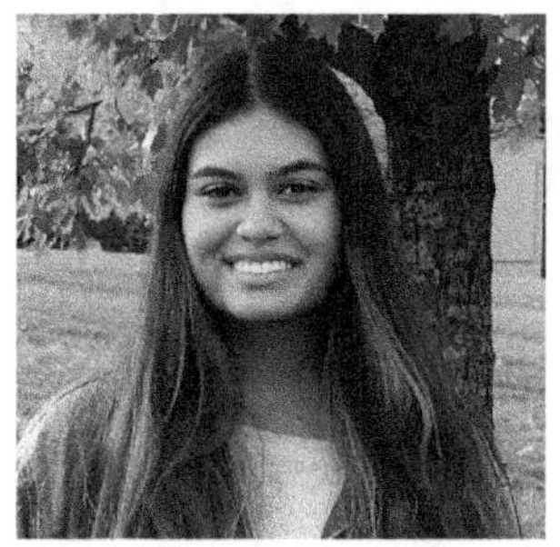

Natasha Yearwood has showcased her work at *The Montgomery Museum of Fine Art.* She will graduate Pace University in 2020 with a degree in Psychology and hopes to attend Medical School.

www.ingramcontent.com/pod-product-compliance
Lightning Source LLC
LaVergne TN
LVHW020640100826
845148LV00012B/2260

* 9 7 8 0 5 7 8 7 9 6 2 1 5 *